Miner's Cottage, Moonta, SA

TREVOR NOTTLE

The Cottage Garden Revived

Attitudes & Plants Essential for
Nineteenth Century Gardens

Kangaroo Press

ACKNOWLEDGMENTS

I would like to pay my respects to these people who have given invaluable help and assistance to me while I have been preparing this book—my wife, Margaret, Tim North, Brian Morley, Rob Swinbourne FLS, Jennifer Stackhouse, Judyth McLeod, Jean Llewellyn, and the Advisory Staff of the Adelaide Botanical Gardens.

My grateful thanks go also to the following people who kindly allowed me to photograph their plants and gardens: Mrs Ethel Venn, Guy Somerton-Smith, Esmond Jones, Lady Law-Smith, Judyth McLeod, Roger Harrop, Mrs Mary Ferguson, Don and Ailsa Salmon, Mrs Betty Pens, Neil Robertson, Tommy Garnett, Iris Hylton and Pat Moulds.

T. J. N.
"Walnut Hill", Stirling

Jacket: A restored country garden—the four essential elements of a cottage garden are evident: profusion of flowers, diversity of plant material, hardiness and simplicity of design.

© Trevor Nottle 1984

Reprinted 1985
First published in 1984 by Kangaroo Press Pty Ltd
3 Whitehall Road (P.O. Box 75) Kenthurst 2154
Typeset by G.T. Setters Pty Limited
Printed in Hong Kong through Bookbuilders Ltd

Hardcover ISBN 0-949924-93-8
Paperback ISBN 0-86417-054-8

CONTENTS

Brugmansia sanguinea

PREFACE

I have, in the following pages, presented some ideas on re-creating nineteenth century cottage and villa gardens—how plants were used, the broad range of plants then available and the attitude of gardeners toward their gardens. Creating the *feel* of a Colonial garden is of the utmost importance in carrying out a garden restoration. I have included as much material as possible from nineteenth century catalogues, papers and books and hope that this will lead readers to make further investigations of their own before beginning work on re-making their Colonial gardens.

Arched gateway with *Rosa fortuneana* and Cordylines, 'Buda', Castlemaine,
Vic.

INTRODUCTION

My aim in writing this book is to share with you my enthusiasm for collecting, growing and enjoying the plant survivors of the last one hundred and fifty years. As the years pass I have managed to devote some time to thinking about how and why such plants have survived, and to how and why these survivors should be kept in cultivation.

In earlier years my first introduction to such fascinating plants was on a more pragmatic plane. I wanted to make a garden, and as a twelve year old I had to make do with cuttings, bulbs, seeds and roots donated by relatives and friends. Even then, being a collector at heart, I wanted to have *new* and different plants which I could show to those adult gardeners who were led on tours of my plot on Sunday afternoons.

My first collections were made walking home from school along back streets and lanes overhung with straggly geraniums and trailing nasturtiums—where are those fantastic dark garnet red shades now? In winter, I was able to pull up clumps of jonquils from the margins of the cabbage fields in the market gardens of our district. I was also able to take slips from fuchsias and scented pelargoniums growing around the old homesteads. An uncle introduced me to a nurseryman who tried to show me how to take cuttings of *Datura* (known as *Brugmansia* in those days) but I failed to catch on. Fortunately, my interest was kept alive by two old ladies who took me on as a gardener's boy. In their splendid garden, complete with pit-conservatory, vinery, potting shed and compost bins, I learned how to garden the *right* way. I also shared with them the pleasures of their flowery domain.

From that time on, I was caught, and read eagerly, beginning with G.S. Thomas, Christopher Lloyd, Peter Coates, the plant hunters and overseas journals; later I discovered Nancy Steen, Alice Coates, William Robinson and all the rest. Along the way, I also learned how to scrounge, an important lesson for any plant collector, as well as the arts of swapping, trading and

—The South Australian Advertiser, p.1, July 12, 1858.

A group of nasturtiums

giving. My collection of plant oddities and curios grew along with my appreciation of their special attractions and quiet beauties.

In those days I was regarded by those who knew me as a teenager with a strange hobby. I gardened, and not only that, I grew the stinking Palestine Lily and Dragon Lily, and dug up roses, bulbs, and other 'old-fashioned rubbish' from footpaths and other public places. Now, I know that there were a good many others doing the same thing, and I'm glad we did for, between us, we kept many good, hardy plants and shrubs going when they could have been so easily lost. For all of you, I hope that this book will be a pleasant journey down a familiar track.

There is another group of gardeners for whom I hope this will be a beginning; they are that enthusiastic band of home restorers who are looking for a few guidelines on what to do about re-making the gardens around their old homes. Here I have made some suggestions about the sorts of plants which were treasured in times gone by and should find a place in our gardens today. But I leave to them the anticipation and pleasure of following up my ideas with their own researches, delvings, scrounging and swap-sessions. For it is by these processes that they will be drawn into the fellowship of plant collectors in their community, sharing with them a deeper appreciation of the beauty and value of old-fashioned plants.

A selection of plants from Alexander Macleay's garden, Elizabeth Bay House, Sydney—late 1840s.

Modern botanical and common names have been given where appropriate. Many of these are still available today.

Ailantuus glandulosa (Tree of Heaven)
Aloysia citriodora (Lemon Verbena)
Alsophila australia (a native tree fern)
Amaryllis candida
Ardisia crenata
Aucuba japonica
Azalea indica
Azalea phonecium
Bauera rubioides
Benthamia fragifera
Bilbergia iridifolia
Butia capitata
Buxus sempervirens (Box)
Camellia japonica
Caryota urens
Cedrus deodora
Chimonanthus fragrans
Cheiranthus mutabilis (wallflower)
Chrysanthemum
Chrysophyllum cainito
Cinnamonum camphora (the Camphor Laurel)
Citrus nobilis (Emperor or King Mandarin)
Citrus aurantiifolia (lime)
Coryphia umbraculifera (Talipot palm)
Cycas circinnalis
Cyclamen persicum
Cocos nucifera (Coconut palm)
Dimocarpus Litchi (Litchi)
Doxantha capreolata
Eriostemon (Wax-flower)
Epidendron (Crucifix orchid)
Erythrina indica
Erythrina crysta-galli (The Coral Tree)
Escallonia rubra
Euonymisis japonica
Euphorbia Jacquinaeflora
Fuchsia magellanica
Gardenia radicans
Gladiolus praecox
Gloxinia youngii

Heliotropium peruvianum (Cherry Pie)
Holmskioldia sanguinea (Chinese Hat Plant)
Iris susiana (Mourning Iris)
Lachenalia flava
Lilium superbum
Linum flavum
Lippia montevidensis
Lonicera japonica (honeysuckle)
Magnolia Michelia Figo (Port Wine Magnolia)
Magnolia purpurea
Magnolia yulan
Mangifera indica (Mango)
Maranta
Nerium (Oleander)
Nyssa aquatica (Cottom Gum)
Osmanthus fragrans
Oxalis bowiei
Plumeria acuminata (Frangipani)
Plumeria alba
Prunus laurocerasus (Cherry Laurel)
Pyrus japonica alba
Quercus virens (Live Oak)
Rhapis flabelliformis
Rhododendron arbureum
Ribes speciosum (Flowering Currant)
Rosa Bracteata (Macartney Rose)
Rosa noisette
Rosa banksiae
Sabal minor (a palm)
Sarcochilus falcatus
Sparaxis tricolor
Spathodia semulata (South African Tulip Tree)
Thuya orientalis
Viburnum tinus
Watsonia rosea
Wistaria sinensis
Yucca aloifolia
Zephyranthes candida
Zephyranthes rosea

By permission of Jennifer Stackhouse, Assistant Curator, Elizabeth Bay House, Sydney.

A garden of roses and hardy plants

1 The Nineteenth Century Gardener
Attitudes towards gardening

The hardest part of planning any garden reconstruction is not the physical labour, nor the search for the hard-to-find plant: it is to visualise a garden in its youth in 1880. Equally hard to understand and appreciate are the attitudes which motivated those bygone gardeners.

In cottage and villa gardens, visual interest came not so much from diverse architectural and built features such as walls, steps and waterworks as from a prolific and varied planting. Looking at old gardens today, we see only the barest bones of their structure and the toughest, most vigorous survivors. Standing in an overgrown Victorian garden today, it is easy to imagine that it was always thus: vast towering shrubs, overblown and frowzy, backed by dolorous, dusty conifers with an understory of leaf-litter, toadstools and flowerless, scraggy shrublets. It's so easy to let such scenes colour our view of nineteenth century gardens. By and large, we think of folk in those times as being sombre, serious and sober, and looking at their gardens today we frequently see in them a reflection of such values. Such impressions are easily bolstered by everyday commonsense knowledge of Victorian times; their love of mourning jewellery, their fondness for the widowed Queen, their meticulous habit of marking every possible event with some sort of monument and the passion which they devoted to religious enterprises all lead the unknowing to consider the Victorians a rather dull lot. How far from the truth!

To uncover the real Victorian or nineteenth century gardeners, we have to look a little deeper than the evidence offered to our eyes by the geriatric remains of their work which we may find today. A little amateur detective work is a lot of fun and usually leads to a few pleasant surprises.

Starting at the house the first steps are to survey the garden, making notes on what you have to start with in the way of plant life, and to make an approximate plan of any pathways which are in existence. As gardens are liable to change with each new owner, it pays to keep an eye out for telltale signs of paths which may have been turned over to garden. Likewise, be aware that in small gardens the general tendency was to simplify the current fashions and to make changes in small ways; so the star and crescent flower beds in the lawns of large mansions were translated into square and circular beds in cottage and villa gardens. Common signs which may help you to decide on the likely layout of your old garden are clumps of jonquils, agapanthus, belladonnas or other bulbs laid out in rows, or regular arrangements of shrubs, roses or small trees.

Several popular layouts are shown in these diagrams.

Five popular nineteenth-century garden layouts

While these path patterns may have been outlined with tiles, bricks or cut stone, it was far more usual to use rough rocks or hardwood laths laid on edge and held in place by wooden pegs. The most common surfacing was pea-gravel, though bricks, slate and even cobbles were not uncommon in areas where they could be obtained cheaply and easily.

In most cases, it is not too hard to settle on an appropriate path and bed layout, guided by the position of doors and gateways with access to sheds and outhouses, as well as by existing plants. Perhaps this most important decision should be made keeping in mind the basic rule to keep things relatively simple. This is more in keeping with cottage and villa gardens which were usually maintained by their owners and will be within the maintenance time available to gardener-owners of today.

To rediscover the rich diversity of plants which once filled in the spaces between and under these remnant trees and shrubs, we must look to surviving records. Searching the literature and archival records is the second phase of the detective work involved in re-establishing an old garden. The most accessible resources are the major public libraries in each state, where information can be located in a variety of sections. Obvious places to search are the Gardening, Horticultural and Landscape categories. Less obvious places are the State Collections, which try to assemble as much material published in the state as possible since publications were first printed, and the archival photographic collections. The libraries attached to Botanic Gardens, Horticultural Colleges and Agricultural Colleges also hold extensive collections of specialised literature. Sometimes local council libraries also hold useful collections related to their community. Historical societies, too, are worthwhile avenues of investigation, particularly as they frequently keep extensive photographic collections and may have accumulated local information based on interviews with old residents or nurserymen.

You should take every opportunity to talk to any old gardeners and nurserymen you may meet so that you can gather your own evidence relevant to your own situation. Often these people have records in the form of old catalogues, stock lists and magazines which go back to the early 1900s. Usually they are happy to talk over their memories and show their keepsakes to anyone who evinces an interest.

Second-hand shops are worth rummaging through in your search for material relevant to gardens of the late nineteenth century. Books, postcards, nursery catalogues, gardening magazines, watercolour paintings and sketches, prints and photographs are all worth poring over and thumbing

May 1, 1876.]   THE GARDEN AND THE FIELD.   209

1876.

FLOWER SEEDS.

VEGETABLE, AGRICULTURAL, AND OTHER SEEDS,

OFFERED BY

E. & W. HACKETT,

73, RUNDLE STREET, ADELAIDE.

Great care is taken to supply everything true to name and of good quality, but without guarantee or warranty.

NOVELTIES AND SPECIALTIES.

Alonsoa Linifolia.
Symmetrical and graceful plant, from 1 to 1½ feet, with pretty dark green flax-like leaves, and covered from the base to the summit with innumerable glowing light scarlet blooms.

Alinsoa Myrtifolia.
The height of this plant is from 2 to 2½ feet, the individual flowers are larger than in any other species of this genus, and of more intense scarlet than those of *Alonsoa linifolia*.

Amaranthus Henderi.
Superb new variety; one of the finest in cultivation.

Amaranthus Amabilis Tricolor.
Charming Indian variety, remarkable for long-pointed leaves, forming dense tufts, from 1 to 1½ feet, beautifully shaded yellow, rose, and flame, spotted brown; effect most dazzling.

Anemone Coronaria Flore Pleno.
A fine strain of all shades and colors, and will yield 90 per cent. of semi-double flowers.

Aplopappus Spinulosus.
Very desirable hardy border plant, blooming the first season, neat and compact, with bright yellow flowers.

Begonia Non Plus Ultra.
Bell-shaped dazzling light scarlet flowers, of enormous dimensions, produced in threes, profuse and continuous bloomer, robust habit, fine dark green foliage; far surpasses all hybrids yet raised.

Callirhoe Pedata Nana Compacta.
New compact variety, which forms charming symmetrical bushes, 1 foot high.

Celosia Pyramidalis, "Reid's Perfection."
Is of remarkably vigorous growth, with graceful pendants of bloom of the finest magenta. This extreme brilliancy of color, combined with the effective habit of growth, stamps it as a valuable addition to our decorative plants.

Centaurea Americana Halli.
Showy new variety, with rich deep purple flowers.

Clarkia Elegans.
Double pure white, perfectly double flowers of snowy whiteness, free blooming, fine for beds.

Coleus, "Duchess of Edinburgh."
Hybridised with all the newest varieties. This cannot fail to produce some novel and beautiful forms of Coleus.

Cyclamen Persicum Grandiflorum.
Saved from Wiggins's varieties, to which so many prizes and certificates have been awarded.

Cyclamen Persicum Grandiflorum Giganteum. (NEW.)
Splendid, with beautifully mottled coriaceous leaves and stout flower-stalks, each flower measuring from 2 to 2½ inches in length, with broad petals of great substance, pure white, with fine bold purple eye.

Delphinium Nudicaule.
Splendid scarlet flowers.

Dianthus Viscidus Compactus.
Interesting species, foot high, forming a neat compact tuft, with brilliant red flowers, quite distinct and choice bedding plant.

Dodecatheon Integrifolium.
Fine species, seeds scarce.

Eryngium Leavenworthii.
Striking and handsome annual, with spiny foliage and handsome rich deep violet flower-heads, with metallic lustre, which preserve their color for some time after being cut.

Fenzlia Dianthiflora Rosea.
A new and charming variety of this lovely Annual, with fine rose-colored flowers.

Gaillardia Amblyodon.
Deep cinnabar red, shading to purple, fine and distinct.

Kaulfussia Amelloides Kermesina.
New and showy variety, with lovely carmine flowers, and may be relied upon to come true from seed.

Linaria Maroccana.
Rich red purple flowers, producing during the summer and autumn. 1 foot high; hardy.

Lychnis Haageana Nana Hybrida.
Forms a splendid mass of rich fiery red, most effective and dazzling for beds and ribands.

Lycenis Lagascœ.
Neat foliage and deep red flowers.

Pansy.
Odier's five-blotched, splendid.

Pansy.
Large-flowered, with very large stains; extra fine.

Petunia Grandiflora Venonsa.
From a very select strain, large flowers, deep rosy purple, veined with black.

Petunia Grandiflora Alba.
This must not be confounded with the small white-blossomed *Petunia nyctaginiflora*; it belongs, on the contrary, to the large-flowering sorts, and supplies precisely the color which has been wanting to complete the collection of *Petunia grandiflora*.

Petunia Hybrida Grandiflora Superbissima.
The flowers of this distinguished Novelty arrests the attention of the most casual observer; the large splendid throat which extending to the middle of the flower is sometimes pure white, most times, however, it is more or less magnificently veined, whilst the flower itself shining in brilliant rose crimson, which reflect a metallic tinge, and contrast charmingly with the fine fresh green of the recurved leaves; it is most vigorous in growth.

Pelargonium.
Large-flowered Exhibition, varieties of Foster, Hoyle, &c.

Pelargonium.
Fancy Exhibition flowers, first-class quality.

Pelargonium.
Perpetual flowering, hybrids of species fine for bedding.

Pelargonium.
Ivy-leaved section, mixed varieties.

Pelargonium.
Tricolor or Variegated-leaved, Gold and Silver-leaved, choice,

A page from an 1876 seed catalogue

'Walnut Hill' Stirling, SA with *Verbascum olympicum*

Rustic Arch and gateway, 'Heide' Bulleen, Vic.

through for items of interest. Among all the junk there may well be some really useful items showing garden details and plant types.

The outcome of all this intense activity will be threefold. The first thing to strike you will be the ease with which you will be able to come to a decision about the style of your garden restoration. All the time you have been busy observing, listening and generally keeping alert to things historical and horticultural, your mind's eye will have been formulating a composite picture of the completed project: considering, rejecting or accepting the information you uncover.

The second thing to happen will be that you are drawn slowly but certainly into a select group of gardeners. As you search, talk and look about you will hear of and meet others engaged in the same pursuit. Like gardeners everywhere you will soon be comparing notes, exchanging plants and striking up new friendships.

The third and most important outcome will be the realisation of the floral richness which existed in gardens in nineteenth centry Colonial times. The most obvious evidence of this will be found in nursery catalogues and garden magazines of the period. To begin with, magazines such as the *Gardener's Magazine*, the *Gardener's Chronicle*, the *Floricultural Cabinet*, the *Garden and the Field* and *Gardening Illustrated* were widely circulated, even as far afield as the Antipodes, and available at popular prices. Scarcely an issue appeared without at least passing reference to the newest plant arrivals from faraway Japan, China, Tibet, Peru, Patagonia, Siberia or Australia. So great was the interest in these new discoveries that the plant-hunters found a profitable sideline in writing narratives of their expeditions. Today these books still make absorbing reading and are keenly sought by collectors. Even the home amateurs got into the plant collection game and the correspondence columns of these horticultural papers are full of letters from folk recently returned from Greece, Italy, the Bahamas, the Alps or the Pyrenees laden with all manner of botanical foundlings which they transplanted to their gardens, with mixed success. This floral explosion was not limited, as we so often and fondly think, to England. Similar, though perhaps less pervasive, forces were at work in the homelands of the other colonial powers, France and Germany.

The seemingly endless flow of seeds, bulbs, tubers, roots and plants was received by the big nurseries and wealthy private collectors, who subscribed to the plant-hunting expeditions in return for a share in the floral booty; but it was usually not long before the hardy plants among them were propagated and distributed widely. Whether given away by generous amateurs, peddled by travelling journeymen from the big nurseries or even filched by the garden staff on the big estates, the treasures of Cathay, Nippon and other distant places were in a few short years widely distributed in the gardens of keen florists.

Parallel to this rapid expansion of available plant species was the development of plant breeding. By today's standards of knowledge, nineteenth-century plant breeding was crude and unscientific, but the pollen-daubers of those days knew that by cross-pollinating two different plants in the same genus, improved forms could be obtained. The number of such improvements was quite staggering, as may be seen by perusing the seedmen's catalogues of the period. From abutilon to zinnia via ferns, geraniums, asters, violets, lilacs, clematis, all manner of alpines, roses, shrubs and trees, the home gardener could select from hundreds of species and cultivars. Not only in floral lines did the nurseries offer an enormous choice, but also in fruit and nut trees, soft fruits and vegetables, with hundreds of apple and pear cultivars and dozens of gooseberries and cabbage strains to choose from.

For the wealthy, with glasshouses and heated stoves (hothouses), there were equally impressive selections in tropical and semi-tropical plants, but as these have no place in a cottage or villa garden, we will not worry about them further here.

The technology of the age played its part in the rapid expansion of the horticultural trade. New techniques made sheet glass much cheaper, and coupled with the new engineering skills of prefabrication and large-scale metal casting, the mass production of glasshouses was possible in a range of sizes from the Crystal Palace (1851) down to small coldframes. New mining techniques produced cheap coal which could be burned to produce steam-heated conservatories and vast propagating houses. Improved transport over

Budding's Patent Lawn Mower

Breen's Patent Finger Spade

Hughes' Aphicide, or Spray Diffuser

the new railway systems and better postal services allowed plants to be delivered safely over long distances. The domestic gardener benefited from all these improvements in having access to many new and comparatively cheap plants. There were also direct technological benefits in the form of numerous handy inventions to make the home gardener's chores easier—the most famous being Budding's Patent Lawn Mower (1830). There were many others too, including all shapes and sizes of sprayers, puffers, secateurs, saws and implements of amazing design for just about every garden operation, e.g. Breen's Finger Spade.

Alongside all these improvements, subsidiary industries arose as by-products from the new heavy industries to support the gardener with chemical fertilisers (slag and coke breeze, nitrates, etc.) and chemical insecticides, fumigants and fungicides. Expanded world trade also brought about the ready availability of such wondrous stuff as Peruvian guano, Abrolhos guano, Colonial guano and even Kangaroo Island guano. The marvels of the Polynesian Rock Phosphate and Superphosphate of Lime produced by the Colonial Sugar Co. (1890s)* were new additions to the home gardener's battery of aids. With such an array at hand, was it any wonder that horticulture flourished as never before?

Of all the inventions which cumulatively allowed rapid horticultural progress in the last half of the nineteenth century, one in particular is frequently held up as the acme of simplicity and timeliness; it was the Wardian Case—a simple, tight-closing miniature glasshouse. Within its comfortable atmosphere, plants and bulbs could be safely transplanted over oceans and continents free from the dangers of death by salt poisoning and dehydration. Originally devised as a means of growing things indoors free from contamination by the soot and grime of London, its broader applications soon became evident to nurserymen and importers keenly aware of the need to minimise expensive plant losses on voyages from the Far East, the Americas and the Antipodes. The full story of Nathaniel Ward's invention has been told in many other books (Richard Gorer's *The English Flower Garden* is one) and need not be repeated here.

Although the stories tell how devices were used to bring plants gathered from all corners of the globe to the major European cultures of the day, very little is told of the reverse process by which the new discoveries were distributed to the settlers in the colonies. Yet the return trade must have been fairly considerable as nursery catalogues from both America and Australia featured many newly raised hybrids and new species, and there is no reason to doubt that similar lines were available in New Zealand, South Africa and Canada, though climate would have modified the choices made by Colonial plant importers. Roses from Germany, France and England were imported in hundreds of varieties, along with French clematis, lilacs and paeonies, and English breeders sent out hundreds of rhododendrons, azaleas, pelargoniums and fuchsias to populate the colonists' gardens.

Towards the end of the nineteenth century, as towns and cities grew larger and reticulated water supplies were established, lawns became more common. Previously, only very magnificent establishments could boast a genuine greensward; others made do with roughly-scythed native pasture grasses which browned off in dry seasons. Most people preferred to use their garden plots for more important and favourite plants such as vegetables, fruit trees and treasured flowers. The arrival of piped water happily coincided with the introduction in Australia of hardy perennial grasses from South Africa and the two events enabled gardeners to plant patches of grass in areas

*My earliest record is *The Garden and The Field*, May 1887, in an advertisement for C.F. Newman's Nursery.

Dr Nathaniel Ward's Closed Case (1843)

too hot and dry for fine turf. Couch, buffalo grass and kikuyu were widely advertised and hailed as a major development for gardeners. A variegated form of buffalo grass was even known, such was the fascination with exotic grasses—if only they hadn't been quite so enthusiastic we should have been saved a great deal of bother eradicating such things as kikuyu grass, paspalum grass and the whole tribe of couch grasses!

Of course, the newfangled lawns needed a swag of gadgetry to keep them going: India-rubber hoses were essential as well as grass shears, scythes and maybe even one of Mr Budding's new hand-propelled, feather-light cast-iron lawnmowers. By and large, lawns still occupied the same shapes which existed previously as garden beds. Towards the end of the period, as lawns took up a larger part of the garden, lawnmower designs improved and they became more widely owned, garden beds became much simpler in shape to make mowing easier. Another aspect of maintenance which helped to simplify garden layout was the need to keep the lawns within bounds. The couch, kikuyu and buffalo grew just as vigorously as they do today and the conventional edgings to beds proved quite ineffectual in containing them. More drastic measures were needed to control such willing growers. There were those who favoured lawns edged with stout jarrah slats to hold in the running grasses, but regular chopping with a hatchet was still needed to keep things under control. A cheaper and more common method was to deeply trench the lawn edges with a sharp spade. The resulting dry moat was considered reasonably effective, even though strenuous hatchet work was still needed now and then to keep the edges neat. Fortunately, we no longer need to use such rampant growers to make a patch of grass, so unless you are really determined to be authentic, the niceties of such hatchet handiwork need not concern you.

The impact of this immense, even staggering, volume of plant material on Colonial gardeners was not to overwhelm them. They took it all in their stride, eagerly welcoming news of the latest discoveries and productions. Each new novelty was enthusiastically received, assessed for the value of its flowers, foliage and habit by the pundits of the day, and assigned a number of potential garden uses in the columns of the horticultural press. Mention might be made here that some of these uses are looked on today as being little more than freakish: multiple grafting and in-arching to produce outlandish specimens, for example. The more extravagant forms of topiary and the excesses of the outlandish bedding-out schemes executed in public gardens and the mansions of the super-rich all draw rather derisive comment in these more enlightened times. But what is important is not what the gardeners of the time did in their gardens with plants but their *attitude* to gardens and plants.

From reading the books, magazines and catalogues of the period the prevalent nineteenth century attitudes towards horticulture were obviously those of enthusiasm, experimentation, and enjoyment in the exuberant use of the floral treasure chest that was being opened by plant-hunters and breeders.

To recapture some of these attitudes must be the aim of any gardener seeking to re-create the atmosphere of a nineteenth century cottage or villa garden. For while the economic strictures of working class life ruled out the wholesale adoption of such grandiose pieces of Victoriana as alpine gardens, pinetums, rhododendron glades, heated conservatories, Chinese gardens and Araucaria avenues, small gardeners nevertheless did make bold, imaginative and colourful use of plants. They were keen to try new plants and acquire as many as their means would allow, displaying them in gay profusion and appreciating them individually. So must follow present-day restorers!

2 The Front Garden

The full impact of diversity and profusion

The most prominent features surviving in front gardens from the nineteenth century are the palms and conifers which were frequently the central forms of their designs. Whether in paired beds or in centrally placed isolation, *Livistona* spp. (Cabbage Tree palm), *Roystonea regia* (Royal palm), *Phoenix canariensis* (Phoenix palm) and even the Date Palm or assorted Araucarias (Norfolk Island pines) or Monkey Puzzle trees formed the centrepieces of relatively formal planting schemes; less frequently other conspicuous trees were used, camellias, dragon trees *(Dracena* spp.) and Wine palms *(Jubea spectabilis)* being quite popular. In favourable areas, rhododendrons might be preferred, while pomegranates were a favourite in warm, drier areas.

No doubt you will have heard horror stories of the expense of removing some of these overgrown monsters from present-day gardens. And not even for the sake of purity would I urge you to plant them today in any but the largest gardens. However, there are a small group of palm-like plants which make authentic and acceptable centrepieces—the Cycads. These grow very slowly, have lovely palmy foliage and were favoured by Colonials and their English cousins as tender pot plants. Like the camellia, we know now that Cycads do not need cossetting in shadehouses. They can be purchased (and they are quite expensive) and planted with confidence, for they will grow slowly and stay a convenient size for very many years. Older rhododendrons and camellias, genuine survivors since the 1880s, can still be found in considerable numbers. By consulting any specialist nursery you should be able to obtain some suited to your needs. Some distinction does need to be made between rhododendrons and azaleas, which were frequently listed as separate entries in catalogues and journals. Rhododendrons were generally

Araucaria excelsa (the Norfolk Island Pine)

regarded as large-leaved, large evergreen shrubs which were generally
limited to the 'hill stations' of Colonial society such as Mt Wilson (NSW),
Mt Macedon (Vic.) and Mt Lofty (SA). Really tough forms such as
Rhododendron ponticum and its many variants were also tried with some success
in favoured suburban locations in Melbourne and Sydney. Azaleas, by and
large, were of the Indica group—low shrubs, semi-deciduous and prodigious
bloomers. Being low growers, they could more easily be found in places of
shelter in suburban gardens than rhododendrons; thus they were widely
cultivated in suburban gardens where soil conditions were acidic.

   If you accept my argument that nineteenth century gardeners enthusiastically cultivated the latest improvements, then you may possibly feel able to
dispense with using only plants from the period and use some modern ones
as well. Before dashing off to indulge in a careless spend-up on the latest
novelties, I should strongly recommend that you consider the form of the
particular flower before you buy. This applies particularly to camellias, and
to roses, which will be dealt with later. These two have been changed
considerably by recent breeding developments. Camellias have become
much bigger and more open, particularly those bred in California and those
bred from *C. reticulata*. These modern blooms would be quite out of sympathy
with the feeling I would be trying to re-create in my old-fashioned period
garden, but you must make your own choice.

Other recent developments in the camellia world, however, might be considered very attractive inclusions in a garden restoration. I have a pair of *C. lutchuensis* grafted on 150 cm standards; their weeping bronzy green foliage and masses of tiny white perfumed flowers seem to be just right. *C. salicifolia* is very similar and would do just as well. *C.* cv. 'Tiny Princess' with pale pink semi-double boutonnieres can also be treated as a standard most successfully. Less well suited, though more freely available, would be *C. rosaeflora*. The growth is too open and foliage too sparse for my liking, however—it doesn't look comfortable enough for the period. The reticulate camellia 'Captain Rawes' was known in nineteenth century times, but it was a great rarity and regarded solely as a cool shade-house resident, or as a large tub plant; I would suggest the inclusion of this type be limited to similar usage in restoration projects.

After all these warnings, don't be put off. There are still hundreds to choose from among the Japonica group: reds, pinks, whites, flakes, parti-coloured, formal, informal, semi-double or single, our grandparents had them all. Their preference was for the formal double, but many others were available. The choice is yours!

In summer gardens and where soil and water were suited, roses were the most popular choice. Of all flowers beloved of nineteenth century gardeners, the rose was surely the best-beloved. Even today we still hark back to the old roses for standards of perfume, charm and cosy homeliness. In our mind's eye we see that Queen of Flowers, the *Rosa perfecta*; an elegantly plump bud adorned with a neatly turned plume of calyx tips which opens to display a rich pink flower tightly packed with hundreds of perfect petals. Layer upon layer will turn back until the fully developed bloom shows us the full beauty of its quartered centre. Nothing but Queen Victoria herself could be more reminiscent of the age.

We are indeed very lucky to have a large selection of nineteenth century roses still available today. They have not always been so, for they fell from grace in the 1920s and were rudely spurned by most rosarians and garden writers of the time. The rapid rise in popularity of the perpetual blooming Hybrid Teas swept all other roses aside. In a few gardens, however, the older beauties were still loved and kept going.

Even way back then, enthusiasts were busy collecting old roses from cottage gardens, churchyards and laneways, a pursuit still popular today. Through Ireland, France and the countryside of England and eastern America, intrepid lady gardeners traversed the lanes and byways ever alert for a glimpse of some ancient rosy treasure. Lovingly transplanted and shared around, they have come down to us today—a profusion of Moss roses, Gallicas, Albas, Centifolias, Damasks, Burnets and roses of Provence. I rather doubt the accuracy of many of the names they now bear, suspecting that they have been assigned by a process of comparison with illustrations in old books and from the brief descriptions in old nursery lists. Notwithstanding, both the roses and the names are full of the romance of a more gracious age, and their appeal is not lessened by the academic nomenclature arguments tossed around in rose journals by old-rose buffs.

Early in the history of Australia these old rose familiars from the homelands were brought here in great numbers for sale, being listed simply under headings such as: 'Moss roses—assorted colours; Damasks, Albas, etc. ditto.' Intending purchasers were usually invited to specify colour preferences or to leave the selection up to the nursery's skilled staff—on whose expertise in all the latest creations ladies and gentlemen could confidently rely.

After the 1860s, catalogues began to list larger and larger selections of the new classes of roses bred from new introductions from China. Boursaults, Hybrid Perpetuals and Teas were the main groups which caught the eyes of the gardening enthusiasts. The main attractions of these new classes of roses were the vastly increased colour range, which for the first time included shades of flame, orange and coral, and the repeat-blooming habit of some cultivars.

The old European varieties, by and large, made rather compact thickets from one to two metres in height (e.g. Gallicas, Burnets) or taller open shrubs (Damasks and Centifolias) which could be planted in hedge-like banks or as specimen flowering shrubs. Often plants were grown as standards or half-standards, but as they were comparatively expensive, it's unlikely they were much used in cottage gardens unless the owner was able to do the budding. The new introductions, Bourbons, Hybrid Perpetuals, etc., were more like modern roses in their growth patterns and habits. The significant difference was that many of the older roses had long willowy canes, where the roses of today have a more compact, erect habit.

This difference meant that the old roses could be grown in a variety of ways which would have given gardens an appearance quite foreign to modern rosarians. The long flexible canes could be trained around posts to make pillar roses; they could be spread low and tied down to pegs—a procedure known as pegging down; or the long canes could be interwoven to create a series of loops. The object of this variety of treatments was to produce flowering stems from most of the dormant buds along the canes. Of course, many roses were grown as regular bushes and standards too.

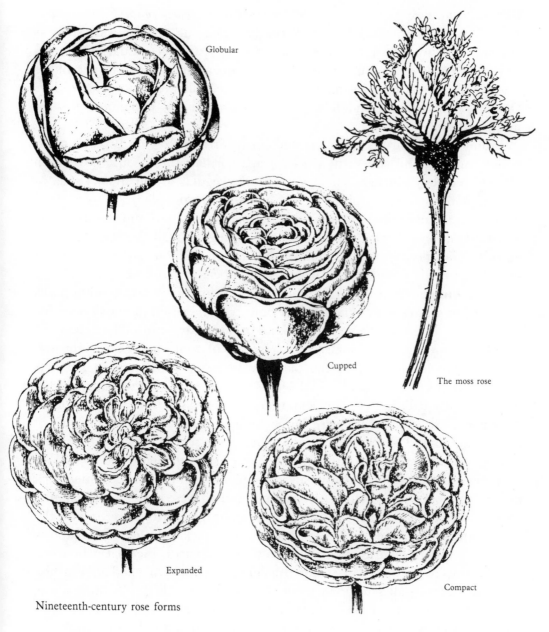

Globular

Cupped

The moss rose

Expanded

Compact

Nineteenth-century rose forms

Besides roses and rhododendrons, the front garden was frequently populated with a wide selection of flowering shrubs, perennials, bulbs and annuals. Whether displayed in the packed profusion of a simple cottage garden or in the more formal setting of a villa garden, the planting was usually more varied in foliage, colour and mix than is usual today. Planted with the shrubs could be found datura, in white, rosy orange and lilac; and fuchsia, especially the shrubby species such as *F. magellanica, F. arborescens, F. cordifolia, F. boliviana, F. corymbiflora alba* and the new hybrids such as 'Erecta Novelty', 'Swanley Gem' and 'Swanley Orange'. Lilacs were also extremely popular, with many new hybrids appearing towards the end of the century; by and large the same cultivars are the mainstream varieties today. Deutzia, philadelphus, buddleja and sambucus were also popular choices for interplanting.

Around these shrubs were planted an assortment of hardy perennials, bulbs, annuals and sub-shrubs. In cottage gardens these could have been planted higgledy-piggledy, or in very simple regular arrangements such as ribbon planting or block planting. In the latter two the plants, all of a kind, were planted out in lines or blocks in a manner still seen in some public parks and gardens. In villa gardens the style of planting generally leant towards the more formal; perhaps a reflection of the current fashion for the Italianate, which was made popular by Victoria and Albert at Osborne.

Some comment here on bedding-out may be instructive. In the big parks and private estates huge quantities of flowers were raised in glasshouses for the purpose of setting them out as a kind of floral carpet to make a dazzling display. Flowering was usually timed by use of controlled heat, light and water in the hot-houses, as the plants were usually wanted, in all their stunning perfection, for peak social events such as gala race meetings, garden parties and debutantes' presentations. Everyday flowers (see C.F. Newman's list on page 22) were raised by the tens of thousands in some of the big houses and municipal gardens. These were set out in carefully studied designs such as scrolls and curlicues, the pattern being heightened by the use of numerous tender semi-tropical 'dot' plants. Tuberous begonias, rex begonias, tubbed aloes, yuccas, cordylines and agaves, alocasia ('elephant's ears'), coleus, caladiums, dracaenas and asparagus ferns were among the most popular and were laid out in endless arabesques with the aid of patterns reproduced in gardening magazines. In some instances, the spaces between the plants were filled with all manner of coloured rock, broken glass, crushed brick and shells—all set out in meticulous patterns. All this fiddliness was beyond the ambition of the cottage and villa gardeners of the colonies, who doubtless would have been far too busy earning a living to bother with such time-consuming labours, labours made even more time-consuming by the need to completely change the plants at least three times a year. William Robinson, the English horticultural writer and publisher, lead a crusade against these tortured and unnatural public plantings, arguing vehemently for a return to the use of hardy plants such as had been grown all along by cottage gardeners. He did not, however, advocate the banishment of annuals such as petunia and lobelia (which in modern usage we know as 'bedding plants').

It was not so much the plants that Robinson was against as the way in which they were used—the amount of labour involved and the hot-house mentality of the gardeners and owners who espoused bedding-out. Descendants of many of these plants can still be found today, but rarely in the separate colour strains which were then available. Among these plants would be a selection of these from the list taken from C.F. Newman & Son's catalogue of 1898 on page 22.

When it comes to choosing from the annuals available today to plant out in a reconstructed colonial garden, there is little point in trying to buy the varieties known in the age of Queen Victoria, for almost certainly few named strains have survived. There is, however, ample evidence from old seedlists that there were many parallels with the seed-lines available today in the old plant families. In petunias, for instance, there were double, frilled, pendant, brush-throated and colour strains just as there are today. Dianthus and picotees are a little more difficult, and the perennial sorts will have to be sought from specialist nurseries dealing in cottage plants and herbs. The annual picotees can usually be bought from nursery outlets and seedsmen. You will not be able to get the old named seed strains such as 'Crimson Belle', 'Mourning Cloak' or 'Pheasant Eye', but you will be able to get modern equivalents of these frilled, laced, eyed and deeply cut flowers. It is more than anything else a matter of keeping your eyes open and getting slips,

Picotee

Double-fringed petunia

FLOWER SEEDS.

Abronia	30	Dolichos	41	Mimulus	48
Acroclinium	30	Dusty Miller	41	Mina	12
Adlumia	30	Eccremocarpus	41	Mirabilis	48
Ageratum	30	Edelweiss	42	Monkey Flower	48
Agrostemma	30	Erpetion	42	Moon Flower	12
Alonsoa	30	Erysimum	42	Morning Glory	49
Alyssum	30	Eschscholtzia	42	Musk	49
Amaranthus	31	Everlastings	60	Myosotis	49
Ammobium	31	Feverfew (see Matricaria)	47	Nasturtium	49
Anagallis	31	Forget-me-not (see Myosotis)	49	Nemesia	49
Anchusa	31	Foxglove (see Digitalis)	41	Nemophila	49
Antigonon	31	Gaillardia	42	Nicotiana	49
Antirrhinum	31	Gazania (see Novelties)	9	Nigella	49
Aquilegia	31	Gentiana	42	Nolana	49
Arnebia	31	Gerardia (see Novelties)	9	Nycterinia	49
Asparagus	31	Geum	42	Oenothera	49
Aster	32	Gilia	42	Pansy	50
Auricula	32	Gloxinia	43	Passiflora	50
Balsam	32	Gnaphalium	42	Peas, Sweet	51
Balsam Apple	33	Godetia	44	Pentstemon	52
Balsam Pear	33	Gomphrena	42	Perilla	52
Bartonia	33	Graderia (see Novelties)	9	Petunia	51
Begonia	33	Grasses, Ornamental	42-58	Phaseolus	52
Bellis	33	Habrothamnus	44	Phlox	52
Beet, Ornamental	33	Heartsease (see Pansy)	50	Picotee	53
Brachycome	33	Hedysarum (see Honeysuckle)	45	Pink	52
Browallia	33	Helianthus	44	Polyanthus	53
Bryonia	33	Helichrysum	44	Poppy	53
Calampelis	33	Heliotrope	44	Portulacca	53
Calceolaria	33-34	Hesperis	44	Primrose	53
Calendula	34	Heuchera (see Novelties)	12	Primula	53-54
Californian Tree Poppy	54	Hibiscus	45	Pyrethrum	54
Calliopsis	34	Hollyhock	45	Rhodanthe	51
Campanula	34	Honesty	45	Rhodochiton (Novelties)	11
Candytuft	34	Honeysuckle	45	Rheum	54
Canary Bird Flower	34	Humulus	45	Romneya	54
Canna	35	Iberis	45	Saintpaulia (Novelties)	10
Canterbury Bells	35	Ice Plant	45	Salpiglossis	54
Cape Forget-me-not	35	Impatiens (see Novelties)	12	Salvia	54
Cardiospermum	35	Indian Shot (see Canna)	35	Sanvitalia	54
Carnation	35	Indian Pink	45	Saponaria	55
Castilleja	35	Inula ensifolia (see Novelties)	12	Scabiosa	55
Celosia	35-36	Ipomaea	45	Schizanthus	55
Centaurea	36	Ipomopsis	45	Sensitive Plant	55
Cerastium	36	Jacobaea	45	Sidalcea	55
Chamaepeuce afra (Novelties)	9	Joseph's Coat (see Amaranthus)	31	Silene	55
Cheiranthus	36	Kaulfussia	45	Snapdragon	55
Chinese Primrose (see Primula)	53	Kenilworth Ivy (see Linaria)	46	Solanum	55
Cherry Pie	36	Lady's Slipper (see Balsam)	32	Spartium	55
Chrysanthemum	36-37	Larkspur	46	Spergula	55
Cineraria	37	Lavatera	46	Statice	55
Clarkia	37	Lathyrus	46	Stipa	55
Clematis	37	Leptosiphon	46	Stock	56
Clianthus	37	Linaria	46	Sturt's Pea	56
Cobaea	37	Linum	46	Sultan, Sweet	56
Coleus	38	Lobelia	46	Sunflower	56
Collinsia	38	Lotus	46	Swan River Daisy	56
Columbine (see Aquilegia)	31	Love-Lies-Bleeding	46	Sweet William	56
Convolvulus	38	Love-in-a-Mist	46	Thunbergia	56
Coreopsis	38	Lunaria	46	Torenia	56
Cornflower (see Centaurea)	36	Lupinus	47	Tritoma	56
Cosmea, or Cosmos	40	Lychnis	47	Tropaeolum	56
Cowslip	40	Malope	47	Trumpet Flower	57
Cuphea	40	Marigold	47	Tydea	57
Cyclamen	39	Marvel of Peru	47	Uniola	57
Cynoglossum	40	Mask Flower	47	Venus' Looking Glass	57
Dahlia	40	Mathiola	47	Verbascum	57
Daisy (see Bellis)	33	Matricaria	47	Verbena	57
Daisy, Swan River	40	Maurandia	47	Vinca	57
Datura	40	Melianthus	47	Violet	57
Delphinium	40	Mesembryanthemum	48	Virginian Stock	57
Devil in the Bush	40	Michauxia	48	Viscaria	58
Desert Pea	40	Mignonette	48	Virgin's Bower	57
Dianthus	40-41	Mimosa	48	Wallflower	57
Digitalis	41			Whitlavia	58
				Xeranthemum	58
				Zea	58
				Zinnia	58

After C.F. Newman & Sons' catalogue of 1898

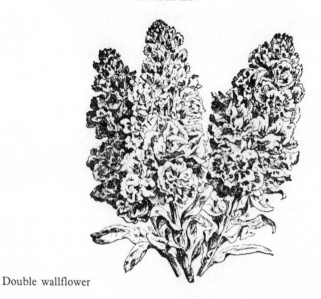

Double wallflower

seeds, etc. of whatever plants meet these descriptions as you visit the gardens of friends and strangers!

Other popular flowers were sweet william, wallflowers, clarkia, godetia and sweet peas, which were all available in separate colour strains. Of these, only sweet peas can still be had in separate strains, such as the 'Gawler' strains, originated by the Harkness family of South Australia. China asters were also much favoured. Varieties such as 'Betteridge's Quilled', 'Boltze's Dwarf Bouquet' and 'Truffaut's Paeony-flowered Perfection' (Improved) were popular in the 1880s. Today's gardeners would be lucky to find more than one strain available. You must look to the big overseas seedhouses if you wish to improve your selection beyond that available from stands of summer seedlings.

Zinnias with names such as 'Tom Thumb', 'Double Striped', 'Dwarf Double' and 'Zebra Zinnias' tell us that Colonial gardeners used a more varied range of forms than are usual today, though the smaller *Z. linearis* and 'Mexicana' strains would make likely substitutes.

One particular group of flowers, classed by gardeners of the 1800s as 'florists' flowers', has not been mentioned. These were flowers grown for display in cool glasshouses, such as are still to be seen in spring and early summer in some public gardens. Among the most popular plants for these purposes were cinerarias, primulas, mimulus, gloxinias, cyclamen and calceolarias. Although amateurs no doubt included some of the hardiest of these in their gardens they were largely the province of professional gardeners and therefore not really fitted to cottage gardens.

One florists' flower was universally popular with exhibitors, professional gardeners and cottage folk alike; it was the pansy. The enthusiastic Colonial gardener could select from a treasure chest of superlative strains: 'Bugnot's Superb Blotched Exhibition', 'Non Plus Ultra', 'Giant Trimardeau', 'King of Blacks', 'Cardinal', 'Gold Lace' and 'Silver Edge', to name but a few. Happily, pansies seem to be making something of a comeback, especially among the tufted violets (now called violas), where you can find 'Bowles Black', 'Maggie Mott', 'Prince Henry', 'Prince John', 'Blue Gem', 'Chantryland' and the modern 'Space Crystals' strain in yellow, blue, white and apricot. The bigger pansies, too, are enjoying a vogue, with at least half a dozen different sorts to choose from at many nurseries. It is hardly of great import, but nonetheless interesting, to ponder whether or not the present 'Butterfly' (or 'Papillon') strain is a descendant of 'Bugnot's Super Blotched Exhibition' or 'Cassier's Very Large Flowered Blotched' or some similar form.

Bulbs, too, played their part in making the show which Colonial gardeners were so keen to see. They were especially valued for their hardiness in the drier areas, and everywhere much admired. This was especially true for bulbs from the Cape of Good Hope. Babianas, ixias, sparaxis, tritonias, watsonias, freesias, belladonnas, nerines and veltheimias were regarded in the Old World as tender subjects, yet in the Antipodes they grew perfectly well outside, multiplying and flowering with a freedom unknown in the Old World. Even such rarities as Elephant's Tongue *(Haemanthus)* and the Cartwheel Lily *(Brunsvigia josephinae)* could be grown to perfection outside.

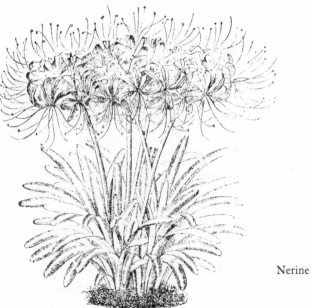

Nerine

Walled garden, Balmain, NSW

Tree camellias and old roses, 'Walnut Hill', Stirling, SA (*Rosa pomifera duplex*—Wolley-Dodds Rose)

Informal borders with old roses and perennials, 'Honey-suckle Cottage', Grose Vale, NSW (Rose × 'M. Tillier')

Gravelled path with clipped box-wood edging, 'Buda', Castlemaine, Vic.

Other much loved South Africans were the agapanthus, which came in several shades of blue and white as well as a silver variegated form and a gold variegated form (now very rare). There were also dwarf forms, a double blue, a pinkish form and a deep blue deciduous form. Naturally these were all blessed with Latin names, but great is the confusion of them, so I won't add to it. Nonetheless, most are still to be had if you look for them, although the double blue seems to be only a name nowadays.

Cliveas and strelitzias were other popular South African 'almost bulbs' which were well known to Colonial gardeners. In those days, cliveas were called *Imantophyllums* and a rare cream form and one with cream margins around the leaves were known to enthusiasts, as well as the well known apricot and orange forms.

A beautiful bulb not often seen these days is *Galtonia candicans*—the Summer Hyacinth. In the 1860s it was recommended to gardeners then for its 'elegant, pure white, bell-shaped flowers'. It is perfectly hardy and easy to multiply from seed.

One last South African family of bulbs must be mentioned—the gladiolus tribe, a wide and varied group very different in the nineteenth century from the tall spikes of symmetrical ruffled flowers we know today. Among the varieties in trade in the last century are a few which can still be found today, though you are more likely to find them growing naturalised along the roadside than in the catalogues of gladiolus specialists! Some are very colourful, others curious, but all are hardy; they include *Gladiolus byzantinus* (bright purple), *G. colvillii* (lavender), *G. colvillii rubra* (brilliant red), *G. colvillii* "The Bride" (pure white), *G. tristis* (greenish) and *G. undulatus* (spidery green).

South America was represented by Jockey's Caps *(Tigridia* spp.) in brilliant colours, Sacred Lily of the Incas *(Ismene festalis)*, the brilliant blue Walking Iris *(Neomarica)* and from Mexico came the dahlia—already highly developed in the nineteenth century, firstly by the French and then by the British.

Bulbous treasures poured out of Chinese, Indian and Japanese ports, sealed in barrels of moss or sawdust for the long voyages to England or Australia. The choice is hardly any greater now than it was in the 1890s when gardeners could choose *Lilium auratum, L. tigrinum* and its double form, *L. lancifolium rubrum* and *album* (now *L. speciosum*), as well as lesser things such as iris, funkia (syn. Hosta) and Hemerocallis. An earlier introduction from India was the Canna, which had been extensively hybridised in Europe—to the stage where catalogues in faraway Australia could boast in excess of forty

Double tiger lily

Cactus dahlias

Lilium lancifolium

Canna

named sorts. Customers were advised that 'fine colour plates of these [Cannas] could be seen on application.'

European bulbs were immensely popular and some would seem highly desirable now, e.g. the range of double hyacinths—black, dark blue, porcelain blue, scarlet, pink, rose, red, white and yellow—all available as named varieties. Tulips could be had in variety, in 'Single Early', 'Early Doubles', 'Show' ('Byblomen', 'Bizarre' and 'Rembrandt', all striped groups) and 'Parrot' classes. In 1889, prices in Newman's catalogue were all four shillings per dozen for named sorts, or 2/6 per dozen mixed.

The Madonna Lily *(Lilium candidum)*, the very essence of a cottage garden ("Where else would they grow?" was the oft-heard wail of gardeners of the upper classes), is still essential today. You may be lucky to find them in a neighbourhood garden or growing wild, especially in the old gold mining districts, or you can raise them easily from seed. Try the Salonika form or the 'Cascade' strain. Solomon's Seal *(Polygonatum vulgaris)* was a popular root for planting in shady areas while tuberoses, Jacobean Lily *(Sprekelia formosissima)* and Vallota Lily *(Vallota speciosa)* were popular for sunny spots. The unusual Pineapple Lily *(Eucomis punctata)* found a favoured spot in many gardens and also made a hardy tub plant. In cooler areas, snowdrops and snowflakes were sentimental favourites too, along with lily-of-the-valley and crocus.

During the middle and later years of the nineteenth century, the daffodil underwent profound changes in the hands of English, Irish and Scottish breeders, and many hundreds of new hybrids were introduced to a receptive and enthusiastic gardening public. A number of readers will no doubt know of places where many sorts of older daffodils can be found naturalised. Collecting bulbs to take home to include in your new re-creation will be easy, but identifying many of them will prove most frustrating—but don't let that put you off an attractive bloom. Jonquils, too, are a very confused group when it comes to names, but are certainly a necessary inclusion in any nineteenth century garden. Among the available jonquils and tazettas (larger and later than the former) are 'Double Roman', 'Paperwhite', 'Soleil d'Or', 'Geranium' (white and red), 'Xerxes' (yellow and red), 'Pleiades' (white and yellow) and 'Silver Chimes' (pure white)—not all genuinely old but every one of them with an air and scent which is purely cottage garden! The main daffodil groups were the large trumpets (Ajax group) of which the double yellow 'Van Sion', 'Bicolor' and the Tenby daffodil may still be had; the medium trumpet group (Leedsii and Incomparabilis groups) with many old doubles such as 'Butter and Eggs', 'Codlins and Cream' and 'Eggs and Bacon', and the small trumpet (Poeticus) group with a host of similar and confusing starry flowered forms still to be found growing in many old gardens.

The other important contributors to the floral tapestry which made up the cottage garden were the perennial plants. So great was their number and such their variety that one hardly knows where to begin. Some have already been listed (agapanthus, hosta, cliveas, etc.), but there were hundreds of other hardy plants to choose from. Picture in your mind's eye a cottage flower border: beginning at the back, some perennial favourites were red-hot pokers (then *Tritomas*, now *Kniphofia*), *Wachendorfia thrysiflorus* (an elegant South African with pleated leaves and tall spikes of rich yellow flowers); *Dietes*, the Butterfly Iris (*D. bicolor*, yellow and brown and *D. iridoides*, white and blue) and Lord Howe Island Wedding Iris (*D. robinsoniana*, pure white and now lost in cultivation, it seems) and the ever popular calla lilies in white, yellow and rose pink. Less common now, but featured in many late nineteenth century catalogues, were *Baptisia* (Wild Indigo), Lavender Shower *(Thalictrum)* and ornamental grasses such as the Zebra Grass *(Miscanthus japonica zebrina)*. For a touch of tropical luxury, unknown in the frosty homelands, tender things such as *Alpinia* (Shell Ginger) and *Hedychium* were available to Colonial gardeners; provided frost-free situations and adequate water supplies could be given, these added a richness of foliage and perfume unseen in European gardens. In the middle of our imaginary herbaceous border of cottagy things were such well-loved favourites as the paeony, asters, shasta daisy, day lily, balloon flower *(Platycodon)*, all members of the iris family (from Spurias to Siberians, Japanese, German, Dutch, English and Spanish), as well as less common things such as Hosta, Globe Thistle *(Echinops)*, *Artemisia gnaphaloides*, *Salvia leucantha*, *S. guaranitica*, *S. uliginosa* and *S. grahamii*. Granny's Bonnet *(Aquilegia)* fitted in the middle ranks too, in shades of rosy-mauve, deep pink, pale pink, dark maroons, purple and white. There were also double forms and a maroon and green form called 'Nora Barlow'. They can still be found today, although being a promiscuous lot, they give very mixed seedlings. In a cottage garden, of course, that is just the effect being striven for.

The front of this marvellous, everblooming border-of-the-mind can be packed with a myriad of colourful delights. Alongside the pansies, picotees, violas, bulbs, etc., already mentioned we will have to poke in just a few Cranesbills *(Geranium sanguineum*, *G. magnificum*, *G. wallichianum* or others), some Alliums (*A. moly*, *A. sicculum*, *A. sphaerocephalum*, *A. albopilosum*, to name a few), the very beautiful *Tovara virginiana*, with leaves brilliantly marked with a rusty red chevron, and maybe some campanulas such as *C. betulifolia*, *C. vidalii* and *C. muralis*.

Having indulged myself in one list, I promise not to overburden you with any more. This small diversion does demonstrate the immense variety of annuals and perennials which were available to gardeners by the end of last century. It was the variety and the profusion with which they were used

Torch lily *(Tritoma uvaria)*

German iris

The giant Japanese iris *(Iris kaempferi)*

which created the special effects, so well loved, of gaiety and abundance in cottage and villa gardens.

A further important feature of last century's gardens was the use of hedges. Hedges came in two sorts, high and hardy, and low and lovely. High, hardy hedges, of boxthorn, olive, hawthorn or laurel were used as boundary markers and were frequently reinforced with thorny additions such as wild roses to keep stock at bay. In really dry areas, cactus hedges of *Opuntia* spp., *Cereus* spp. or *Aloe africana* were used instead, and the prickles of such cacti and succulents were doubtless very effective against browsing cows and horses.

Low and lovely hedges were frequently used to mark major walks and garden beds. Lavender and rosemary were popular choices, but box and ivy were also used, especially where really low decorative designs were carried out. In some low rainfall areas, geraniums made colourful, untrimmed hedges. The problem then, as now, with hedges is that they *will* grow. Being pretty tough is one of the attractions for gardeners starting off from a patch of bare earth and needing quick shelter, but with the toughness goes a considerable willingness to grow vigorously. Trimming hedges is not quite the chore it was in the days before electric shears, but it is still the major drawback facing gardeners wanting to carry out a thorough re-creation. In country gardens especially, hedges still remain; hugely overgrown, often broken through and dead in patches, and a big headache for would-be restorers. Often the obvious choice is to bulldoze the whole wretched assembly, but then you have to decide whether or not to replant it! I won't presume to tell you what to do—the choice is yours. If you do replant a boundary hedge, beware of cypress—it gets very leggy and dies easily. Wild olive seems a good choice to me; it stays well clothed right down to the ground, doesn't need more than an annual clipping and can be rejuvenated by a hard cutting back when needed.

Low hedges inside the garden primarily define major paths or beds or are features in themselves. Aside from lavender, rosemary, box and ivy, low hedges were also made from plumbago, myrtle and wormwood. With advancing old age, all these hedging materials develop patches which collapse or die, or both! Nevertheless, for sentimental and historic reasons, these plants are still the obvious choices for low hedges. One more recent plant which is acceptable in terms of appearance and suitability for clipping is *Lonicera nitida* 'Baggesens Gold': a golden small-leaved shrublet which is much superior to the hayfever-producing Gold Privet!

Informal, unclipped hedges in the form of banks and screens could be constructed from a much wider selection of plants. Among the best choices would be the thicket-forming roses—Spinosissimas, Rugosas, Gallicas and roses of Provence—and the taller shrubby Fuchsias such as *F. magellanica, F.m. Ricartoni* and *F.m. gracilis variegata*. In drier, sunny spots, zonal and Regal pelargoniums would be admirable, remembering though that some of the more startling coloured varieties of modern times are inappropriate historically and aesthetically. Fortunately there are still plenty of genuine old cultivars available through specialist nurseries and societies. Most often, such banks of low shrubs contained a mixture of different forms of the same plant (e.g. geranium), making a hedge of pink, rose, scarlet and white flowers. If need be, the plants could be cut back hard every now and then to trim up scraggy growth and keep the planting compact. Roses grown in such a manner should not be pruned in the regular way; instead, dead and spindly growth should be removed and the remaining canes intertwined with each other. When the new growth commences, it will grow together forming a light but well clothed screen.

The front garden so described presents us with the ideal picture of a nineteenth century garden: a profusion of plants overflowing and softening a simple formal layout, sometimes featuring simple arrangements of plants treated as standards or specimens and underplanted with a rich assortment of annuals, bulbs and perennials; and sometimes featuring an informal planting, even including vegetables, massed together in a casual, comfortable clutter.

Those people restoring a nineteenth century terrace house or semi-detached cottage in an inner-city area will have very little garden area to plant. The pocket-handkerchief front garden presents the biggest challenge to keep up a good display. Doubtless bygone owners would have used annuals puchased in flower, just as present owners will, to make up the main displays. Some permanent features such as perennials and bulbs will need careful attention as to choice, as only a few could be included. Many of you will have your own favourites but may I suggest a few? The Regal Lily (*Lilium myriophyllum* now *L. regale*) is a very lovely and easy bulb which just fits into the period, being first discovered in 1903, though not widely introduced until 1912 when E.H. Wilson made his major collection in the wilds of Szechwan at the Min River Valley. *Lilium candidum* is a splendid choice too, or the Tiger Lily (*L. tigrinum*) or *L. speciosum*. Other bulbs could be clumps of one or two really fine daffodils or tulips. Among perennials, the Bleeding Heart (*Dicentra* spp.), hosta, platycodon and some sort of white daisy would be a representative selection. The important thing is to have really prolific flowering things which are neither invasive nor need frequent replanting. For shrubs I would choose Tea roses, such as the coppery pink 'Monsieur Tillier', a tree paeony or the very beautiful *Cantua buxifolia*. If room permits, more well-known cottage plants such as lavender, herbs and pinks could be included.

It is not possible to have in such a small space the abundance of the larger nineteenth century garden, so on this note we will leave the front garden and proceed to the gardens at the side of the house.

3 The Side Gardens

In shrubbery and shade house

The problem of which side of the garden to enter first can be a delightful choice or a doubtful pleasure, depending on whether your particular piece of the nineteenth century has a 'garden at the side' or a 'side-garden'!

The side-garden is the big problem for any modern urban gardener, and was no less a one for the gardener of yesteryear. What can be done with a space two metres wide and fifteen metres long? By the time the necessary path has made its passage from end to end, there is precious little room left for any sort of gardening. The most common solution to these narrow windtraps has been to ignore them as garden spaces and to treat them solely as utilitarian routes from front to back. In some inner-city areas, such spaces were so small and overshadowed that they were left quite alone—any attempts to brighten them with pots or climbers merely hindered safe passage.

However, the wider spaces that were available to home-owners were frequently converted on at least one side into a shadehouse or a grape-cage. These structures ranged from simple constructions of cheap timber, laths and chickenwire to elaborate confections of fretted timber and turned finials.

The other side of the garden, most often the sunnier side, was frequently developed as a shrubbery or even a small orchard; more energetic households used the space for a bowling green, croquet lawn, badminton or tennis court. In a modern restoration, the wider spaces may be authentically developed in any of these roles, at the same time serving the needs of a family. Some care need be taken, though, not to allow all the modern paraphernalia of tennis to intrude into the nineteenth century feeling of the place—electric lights, en-tout-cas and chainwire backstops would look entirely out of place.

If an orchard is settled on as the object of restoration, you might consider choosing trees beyond the cultivars commonly available through garden centres. Fortunately, comprehensive collections of old fruit trees are still held by some agricultural research stations, particularly of apples and pears. Some keen commercial orchardists also keep 'odd lines', favourite old varieties of dessert and cooking fruits, survivors of the hundreds of cultivars which were offered to the garden makers late last century. In cool and moderate areas, apples, pears, cherries and soft fruits could be the major plantings, with plums, persimmons and even medlars to add variety.

The page from a late nineteenth century catalogue reproduced on page 34 gives some idea of the variety available.

Peaches, nectarines and apricots would also be appropriate, but since some trouble will need to be taken over cultivating these trees anyway, a choice in favour of some of the toothsome varieties of bygone days could be made.

In warmer areas, citrus trees planted in a small grove might appeal as a restoration project. Blood oranges, pomeloes, citrons, shaddocks and limes could be attractive alternatives to the usual oranges and lemons, especially if you remember the flavour of blood oranges or enjoy making marmalades. For drier gardens, a grove of almonds, loquats or even olives could create the feeling of an orchard. To make it especially romantic, you could put in a dense underplanting of jonquils and Cape bulbs.

Should an opportunity present itself, keen gardeners may wish to investigate the mysteries of espalier. Intriguing terms such as *cordon, double*

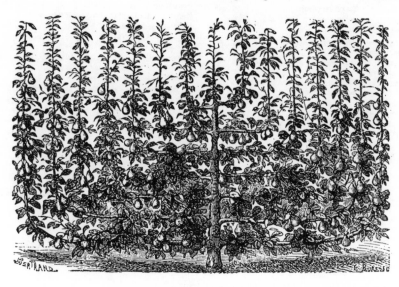

An elaborately espaliered pear tree

208   **E. & W. HACKETT,** Seedsmen, Nurserymen, &c., 73 Rundle Street, Adelaide.

APRICOTS.

1s. each ;   per dozen.

Description.	Season.
Beauge, very large, like *Moorpark,* juicy and rich ...	L
Bush Peach, large, rich, juicy. One of the best ...	M
Campbellfield Seedling, medium size, good ...	M
Carrington, fine large, late variety, bears well ...	L
Dundonald	
Hemskirke, large, roundish, slightly compressed on the sides ; flesh bright clear orange, tender, juicy, and richly flavoured	E
Kaisha, middle size, roundish, skin pale yellow, tinged with red on the sunny side ; flesh yellow, transparent, tender, juicy, and rich	E
Large Early, light-coloured and very rich ...	E
Mansfield Seedling, large, fine flavour	L

Description.	Season.
Moorpark, large, roundish, skin deep orange, marked with brownish red on sunny side ; flesh orange, firm, juicy, and rich. A very excellent variety... ...	M
Oullin's Early Peach, large, juicy, rich, fine flavour. The best early, and a good bearer	E
Red Masculine, small, juicy, musky flavour ; very early	E
Roman, large, abundant bearer	M
Royal, large, skin dull yellow, tinged with red ; flesh pale orange, firm, rich, juicy, and vinous. An excellent variety	M
Shipley's (Blenheim), large, juicy, and rich ; good bearer	E
Warwick, large and excellent, fine flavour	L

ALMONDS.

9d. each :   per dozen.

Brandis   Nonpareil

Jordan   Paper-shell

CHERRIES.

1s. each ;   per dozen.

Description.	Season.
Bedford Prolific (Black), large, much like *Black Tartarian*	M
Belle d' Orleans (White), tender, juicy, and rich ...	E
Bigarreau Early Twyford (Red)... ...	E
Bigarreau Napoleon (Pale Red), large, rich, and good. A most abundant bearer...	L
Black Eagle, large, deep purple, rich, sweet, and most delicious flavour	M
Black Heart, an old favourite, large, heart-shaped, blackish purple	E
Black Tartarian, very large, sweet and good, bright black. A noble-looking Cherry	E
Early Lyons (Black), the largest early Cherry, excellent, and very handsome	E
Early Purple Guigne, large, juicy, dark purple, almost black. A most delicious Cherry	E

Description.	Season.
Early Rivers, large, black, tender, very prolific ...	E
Florence (Red), large, fine flavoured, very firm, juicy, and sweet	L
Governor Wood (Red), large, juicy, and sweet ...	M
Heart of Midlothian (black), fine flavour	M
Kentish, good cooker	
Knight's Early Black, large black, rich flavour ; abundant bearer	E
Mayduke (Red), very prolific, dark red, fine flavour, and good for cooking	M
Morello, large acid ; very useful for the kitchen ...	L
St. Margaret (Black), large, sweet, and firm ...	L
Waterloo (Black), large, tender, and juicy	L
Werder's Early Black, large, tender, juicy, rich flavour	E
White Heart, mottled, sweet, and rich	L

FIGS.

1s. each ; 10s. per dozen.

Black Ischia, large, sweet and rich, skin deep purple. Ripe at Christmas

Black Smyrna, the best for drying

Brunswick, brownish purple, large, rich, and good

Castle Kennedy, large, early, and prolitic

Green Ischia, medium size, fine flavour

Grosse Verte, green, very large, rich and excellent ; late

Turkey, large, fine flavour

White Adriatic, one of the very finest

White Genoa, large and good, very rich ; dries well

White Provence, one of the best. Ripe at Christmas

A page from a late nineteenth-century catalogue of fruit trees *cordon, horizontal cordon, fan* and *in-arching* will become familiar knowledge as almost lost skills are re-learned. These special ways of training and pruning fruit trees do need devoted attention over a good many years to produce the lovely tunnels, fans, urns and allées which can be seen in illustrations of last century's fruit gardens. The only difficulty will be in finding someone familiar with the management techniques of espalier from whom the skills may be learned. The best places to locate such a person would be through state Department of Agriculture research stations, or perhaps the training sections of the botanic gardens in each capital city.

Shrubberies were a popular method of making gardens in the areas to the side of the house and had the added advantage of being considered very fashionable and needing much less labour than the foregoing orchards. As in previous cases, the choice was very wide, with a much greater selection of hardy shrubs from the temperate zones than is generally available today. There was not the emphasis on the semi-tropical plants which are promoted and offered today, and Victorian gardeners did not subscribe to the modern idea that a good garden can be achieved with a minimum of maintenance— people who wanted good gardens expected to have to do some work! So pruning, trimming, training and disease-control activities were seen as part of the gardener's calendar and not as avoidable chores.

Foremost among the shrubs were those evergreen favourites, the lilacs, philadelphus, forsythia, deutzia and spiraea. Fortunately for garden restorers, many of the varieties available today were bred towards the end of the last century, so obtaining these plants is not a difficult task. However, some other shrubs grown during the reign of Queen Victoria are less easily obtained; the spectacularly beautiful Sacred Flower of the Incas *(Cantua buxifolia)* with great clusters of pendant silky carmine flowers, the exotic orange-trumpeted *Datura sanguinea*, the Matilija Poppy *(Romneya coulteri)* with its huge crimped white blooms with golden central bosses, and the majestic Plume Poppy *(Macleaya cordata)* with huge silvered fig-like leaves and tall spires of rusty pink flowers, are among the best. This last plant was named in honour of our own Alexander Macleay and so is doubly appropriate for Australian gardens.

Semi-tropical plants flourished in most parts of the Antipodean colonies and consequently plants which had been regarded as greenhouse subjects in Europe were used here in the open ground. Principal among these were oleander, lantana and bouvardias.

True European evergreens had great sentimental attractions, especially for the traditions attached to Christmas, so box, yew and holly were much

Lantana

A group of bouvardias

cultivated. Among the hollies were several which are worth seeking out: the Hedgehog Holly with strange crests of spines on the upper leaf surfaces—the variegated form is especially good *(Ilex aquifolium horrida* cv. *variegata)*—and the plain variegated sorts 'Milk Maid' (yellow centre and curled green edges), 'Silver Queen' (silvery edges) and 'Golden Queen' (yellow edges). These will all eventually make quite large shrubs so unless you have plenty of room, care will be needed in placing them.

No garden restoration would be complete without scented shrubs for, after colour, perfume is what most of us would call to mind as typical of a cottage garden. Lemon-scented Verbena *(Lippia citriodora)* is a powerfully-scented small tree which is especially useful as it casts light shade and has an easy temperament (though it is frost tender). Rarer, but worth asking after, is *Azara microphyllus* which has minute yellow blooms under the leaves and a rich vanilla perfume. Quite different are Carolina Allspice *(Calycanthus florida)*, Wintersweet *(Chionanthus fragrans)* and the Witch-hazels *(Hamamelis mollis)*. The Bull Bay Magnolia *(Magnolia grandiflora)* is a well known small tree with delightfully perfumed flowers (usually around Christmas), which could be used with any of the above to create the scented atmosphere so necessary for a cottage garden.

At lower levels, the many varieties of scented-leaf geraniums can fulfil the multiple roles of providing varied foliage, rich scents and easy culture. A selection from the thirty or so varieties available from specialist nurseries will satisfy even the most discerning gardener. Among the best are *Pelargonium tomentosum* and *P.* × 'Mabel Grey' (rich lemon scent) with large leaves. Contrasting leaf forms still with powerful perfumes can be had from varieties such as *P. crispum*, *P. abrotanifolium* and *P.* × 'Countess of Stradbroke' (citronella perfume). Less well scented are varieties such as *P.* × 'Scarlet-Pet', *P.* × 'Pink Pet', *P.* × 'White Unique' and *P.* × 'Rollison's Unique' (brilliant red), but they are nonetheless very attractive survivors from the last century.

Butterfly bushes are less common than they used to be and should be more widely planted for their plentiful scented flowers and ease of culture. The form *Buddleja asiaticus* is still fairly common, though often grossly overgrown and in need of a hard pruning, but *B. alternifolia* with graceful wands dotted with small clusters of lilac flowers and *B. globosa* with large round heads of orange flowers dotted along the branches are equally attractive and less common. *Buddleja salvifolia* has a heavier look than the others, having dense foliage which hangs down on branches already weighed down by the large panicles of tiny lilac flowers.

Most treasured of flowers since their introduction from Shanghai in the 1780s on behalf of Sir Joseph Banks, the tree paeonies were available through big nurseries which usually advertised them coyly as 'various varieties'. The colours were usually deep maroon (semi-double), lilac (fully double), pale lilac with a deep basal blotch (almost single) and white. The really sumptuous colours came early in the twentieth century at the hands of French breeders, so they don't strictly fit here, but I would bet any nineteenth century cottage gardener would have jumped at the chance to have one. Such rare beauties are mighty rich stuff for any garden, so tree paeonies should be placed with great care and planted sparingly. If the cost of such treasures puts you off— they are currently between $35-$55 per plant—you can raise them from seed. The disadvantage here is that they take from five to seven years to flower and may well turn out to be fairly ordinary—if any tree paeony can be said to be ordinary!

By way of contrast, three much quieter shrubs which still attract attention in their due season are *Cedronella triphylla*, with its very pungent leaves and compact terminal leads of pale lavender flowers, and *Lonicera ciliata*, in either pink or white forms. All three have simple, plain features—none of the flamboyance of paeonies—and fit well into any sunny corner of a cottage garden. The *Cedronella* is frost tender, so in areas where it gets badly cut back it will perform more like a herbaceous perennial than a shrub. In warm areas, it will easily make two to three metres.

Well, I hear you say, he hasn't said anything about geraniums yet except as hedges—and the scented pelargoniums! I will do so at once. To begin with, I must confess my ignorance of them as I now grow very few. I know that varieties like 'Mr Wren' (red with a fine white edge) and 'Apple Blossom Rosebud' (white double with a greenish centre and rose pink edges) were known and loved way back, and I am sure a geranium enthusiast will be able to show you more lovely varieties from the last century. But to me the acme of Victorian geraniums were the variegated forms in gold, silver and bronze. Whether tricolours or bicolours, their brilliant leaves speak to us still of the Great Exhibition display gardens and cottage doorstep alike. So favoured were these plants that a good many have survived to the present day. I include for your interest the recommended varieties listed by Sewell's Payneham Nursery in 1886:

GOLDEN TRICOLOR AND SILVER TRICOLOR PELARGONIUMS.

Capt. Willett, white margin, brilliant carmine zone. 2s.

Countess of Craven, leaves green, with rich crimson and bronze zone, golden yellow margin. 2s. 6d.

Dolly Varden, very broad bright red zone

Golden Pheasant, rich yellow ground, bronze red zone, green centre. 1s. 6d.

Humming Bird, broad metallic bronze zone, margined with rich crimson. 2s.

Italia Unita, leaves green, zone bright rosy carmine and black, edges white. 2s. 6d.

Lady Cullum, leaf margined bright yellow, with broad irregular zone of red and black, green centre. 2s.

Louisa Smith, leaves margined yellow, fine distinct zone of bright crimson and black, olive-green centre. 2s.

Mrs. John Clutton, distinct white edge, crimson zone. 2s.

Mrs. Pollock, leaves green, bright bronze red zone, belted crimson, golden yellow margin. 1s. 6d.

Mrs. Rutter, leaves olive-green, broad black zone mixed with fiery red, pale yellow margin. 2s.

Sir Robert Napier, yellow, very bright red streak. 2s.

Sophia Cusack, lemon-yellow margin, golden disc, encircled with bright scarlet zone, bronze border

Sophia Dumaresque, bright yellow edge, rich red and black zone ; a good, vigorous grower. 1s. 6d.

Star of India, centre green, surrounded with zone of lake and crimson on bronzed ground ; distinct and beautiful. 2s.

Sunbeam, light yellow margin, dark chocolate zone, splashed with red, green centre. 3s. 6d.

Sunset, margin yellow, bright red zone, very distinct. 2s. 6d.

Wm. Sandy, narrow inflamed scarlet zone, dwarf. 2s.

And others.

GOLDEN, BRONZE, AND SILVER BICOLOR PELARGONIUMS.

1s. 6d. to 2s. each.

A Happy Thought, centre of leaves creamy white, with green margin ; the stems are also white. A very distinct variety. 1s. 6d.

Avalanche, flowers pure white, good shape ; free-flowering, trusses thrown just above the dark green leaves, which are broadly and regularly edged white

Beauty of Calderdale, greenish yellow, with broad chestnut red zone, good bold foliage, free grower. 1s. 6d.

Black Douglas, yellowish green, broad dark chocolate zone, narrow golden edge

Crystal Palace Gem, yellow, green centre. 1s. 6d.

Distinction, rich green leaf, disc circumscribed by a well-defined narrow vandyke zone

Duke of Wellington, pale green leaves, with narrow chocolate zone

Freak of Nature, a great improvement on *A Happy Thought*

Marechal MacMahon, thick bold leaves, with broad well-defined dark bronzy chocolate zone, yellow disc

Mont Blanc, silver-edged foliage, with large pure white flowers. 1s. 6d.

Mrs. J. C. Mapping, leaves green, with very broad creamy-white margin ; flowers white, with pink eye, produced abundantly. 1s. 6d.

Mrs. Parker, bold and finely-variegated foliage, fine double pink flowers

The Shah, deep yellow ground, with broad chocolate zone, large well-formed leaves. One of the best

Waltham Bride, dark green, broad edging of pure white, fine pure white flowers

By checking these lists against those from present-day specialists, you should be able to obtain a good selection and may even be able to identify some you already know. Colonial gardeners had generally been accustomed to think of these fancy-leaved geraniums as pot plants which could be put in the ground for summer display, but it could not have been long before it was found that many of them would grow perfectly happily outside year round. Varieties such as 'A Happy Thought', 'Distinction' and 'Marechal MacMahon' could make quite decent sized bushes if left unpruned.

Passing from this sunny garden gay with geraniums, we now come to the shady side garden where we will almost certainly find some sort of shadehouse. Built rustic style of rough hewn branches and brush, or more properly of sawn timbers and laths, it created a small haven of shade and coolness where ferns, palms and other potted plants could be grown. Under the tender ministration of a housewife or working-man such treasured plants as coleus, begonias, palms, ferns, gardenias and maybe some epiphytic cacti or hardy orchids were grown.

On the damp floor of the bush house grew such old favorites as Baby's Tears *(Helxine)*, Kenilworth Ivy *(Linaria)* or perhaps *Mentha requenii*. Sometimes large pots stood directly on the floor with palms, camellias, hydrangeas, gardenias or other plants which required shelter from scorching sun and drying winds, in special soil. In a dark corner, that epitome of Victoriana, the aspidistra, might well be found. Known everywhere as the Cast Iron Plant, the aspidistra could be relied on to grow almost anywhere so long as it wasn't bone dry! Whether plain or variegated, it was a most obliging plant, at home in parlour or palm-house. I have no doubt its curious bobble flowers, produced at ground level, excited many amateur naturalists and plant spotters. Local ingenuity often showed itself in pots devised from hollow gum logs and crammed with sword-ferns, native Dendrobium orchids *(D. speciosum, D. kingianum, D. delicatum)*, native Cymbidium orchids *(C. canaliculatum, C. madidum, C. suave)* or asparagus ferns such as *A. falcatum, A. sprengerii* and *A. plumosus*. Hanging baskets carved out of tree-fern logs or hollow gum logs by home handymen housed the real treasures of the fernery—the Boston ferns *(Nephrolepis* spp.), the Caterpillar Fern *(Polypodium glaucum)* the fabled Mander's Golden Polypody *(Polypodium aureum mandianum)* or the huge weeping mass of a Jointed Polypody *(P. subauriculatum)*. Among serious pteridologists, a vast range of ferny novelties and rarities were circulated and grown with exacting skill. The Maiden Hair ferns *(Adiantum* spp.) were extremely popular, as can be seen from the 1880s list reprinted on the next page.

	Price.
Adiantum (*Maiden Hair Fern*)—	
Æmulum, a graceful variety, suitable for baskets	2 6
Æthiopicum, light green foliage	1 6
Amabile, a beautiful Fern, producing graceful drooping, light green fronds, suitable for hanging baskets	2 6
aneitense, suitable for baskets	2 6
Bausei, peculiar and ornamental	2 6
***Bellum**, very dwarf and compact, forming neat pretty green tufts of slender fronds, about six inches high ... 1/6 to	2 6
Braziliensis ..	3 6
***capillus veneris**, a pretty and useful species	1 6
***capillus veneris fissum**, leaflets deeply lacerated	2 0
***capillus veneris magnificum**, a very fine variety for cutting ... 1/6 to	2 0
cardiochlæna, makes a fine specimen	3 6
caudatum, long, narrow, arching fronds ; nice for baskets ... 2/- to	2 6
concinnum, most rich and graceful, beautiful for baskets ... 2/- to	2 6
***cuneatum**, very distinct and pretty ; dark green foliage. One of the best for cutting for bouquets, &c. ... 1/6 to	10 0
cuneatum grandiceps, a crested variety of *A. cuneatum* ; attractive in appearance, and well adapted for growing in baskets	2 6
cuneatum mundulum, compact and distinct, leaflet small...	2 6
Cunninghami, a distinct and pretty species 1/6 to	2 0
decorum, a handsome, free-growing variety	2 6
diaphanum, suitable for baskets	2 6
dolabriforme, well suited for baskets ...	2 0
***elegans**, hardy, free-growing ... 1/6 to	10 0
elegantissima (new), very fine	2 6
excisum multifidum, fronds heavily crested	2 6
Farleyense, the most magnificent of this handsome family. One of the finest plants in existence 3/6 to	7 6
formosum, a large handsome free-grower	2 6
gracillimum, this is a charming variety, particularly pleasing on account of its light and graceful appearance, produced by the number of its minute pinnules. Most valuable for cutting. A most elegant and distinct Fern 2/6 to	5 0
gracillimum cristata	2 6
Lawsoni, fine light fronds	2 6
Legrandi, very distinct fronds, dense, leaflets small	2 6
Luddemannianum ...	5 0
Macrophyllum, young fronds rosy crimson ; splendid	2 6
***Mariesi**, very handsome, distinct	2 6
Nobile, handsome ... 2/- to	2 6
Pacotti, fronds small, triangular, dense...	2 6
***pedatum**, an elegant species, free-growing and hardy ; its lovely pellucid fronds are most delightful ... 1/6 to	2 6
Peruvianum, graceful arching fronds, with large leaflets ... 2/6 to	3 6
pubescens ... 1/6 to	2 6
Reginæ	2 6
reniforme, very distinct, kidney-shape foliage ...	2 6
rubellum, young foliage deeply coloured ruby tint	2 6
Sanctæ Catherinæ, large fronds	2 6
scutum, bold and handsome fronds, large	2 6
tenerum, makes a fine specimen	2 6
tetraphyllum	2 6
trapeziforme, a handsome species, producing very long fronds ... 2/6 to	3 6
Veitchi	3 6
Weigandi, very distinct, leaflets cripsy	2 6
Williamsi, a fine-growing species of Maiden Hair, slightly golden underneath the fronds	2 6

A list of maidenhair ferns reproduced from an 1880s catalogue

Pteris, Selaginella (Club Moss), *Asplenium* (Hen and Chickens Fern) and many other curiosities were well known. Native ferns had their advantages, too, especially when many woodgetters and bullockies could hawk them door-to-door in the towns. Hardy and still beautiful tree ferns, shield ferns (*Polystichum* spp.), wild maiden-hair ferns, fishbone ferns (*Blechnum* spp.), Bird's Nest fern (*Asplenium*) and the glorious Elkhorn were brought in from the rainforests and eagerly sought by Colonial gardeners.

The current fern revival has seen many ferns considered highly desirable in colonial times brought back into high favour. Not only rarities such as the Crested Hart's Tongues (*Polypodium scolopendrifolium cristata*, et al) but distinctive commoners like the Sensible Fern (*Onoclea sensibilis*) and the Japanese Painted Fern (*Athyrium goeringianum pictum*).

Gardeners intent on reconstructing any sort of fernery should have little difficulty in obtaining suitable materials—brush, laths, tree-fern logs, etc.— for the job and should be able, with only a little searching, to locate a suitable diversity of hardy ferns. Some care should be taken over the use of some

A group of ferns in a carved wooden planter

modern materials such as nylon shade cloth and trickle irrigation schemes, for marvellous as they are their thoughtless deployment in an old-time structure can totally destroy the illusion you want to create. This is not to say they shouldn't be used, just that they shouldn't be allowed to intrude. This is where the ingenuity of the home handyperson will be put to the test!

After the fern fad, a host of other pot plants were loved and grown by Colonial gardeners. One of the least common and most surprising was *Hibiscus schizopetalus*, with finely cut pendant rose-red flowers. Why it's not more in demand I cannot tell, for it makes a unique plant for a tub in a sheltered corner.

Other highly regarded plants were bromeliads; a seemingly endless variety of the pineapple family was introduced from tropical America. Almost everyone had Queen's Tears *(Billbergia nutans)*, and the purple Zebra Plant *(Billbergia zebrina)* was widely grown. Even Spanish Moss *(Tillandsia* spp.), that curious grey wispy stuff (also known as Air Plant) was fondly treasured in many a shadehouse. There are many variegated and highly coloured members of this family, including *Neoregelia, Nidularium, Aechmia, Ananas* and *Dyckia* which would have been known to enthusiasts and desired by many.

The Wax Flower *(Hoya carnosa)* was another pot plant whose scented bunches of white waxy blooms made it an attraction for every pot-gardener. There were rose-pink forms as well, and at least one with variegated leaves.

Much smaller in all respects is *Hoya bella*, as popular then as it is now. There is also *Hoya australis*, which would have been brought from its rainforest habitat by plant collectors and sold to nurseries for resale. Its sharply reflexed blooms gave it the popular name of Starry Wax Flower. All these and many more are still to be found in succulent collections and appear from time to time at plant sales. Every colonial dame knew that Hoyas need very little root room and that flowers come on the same stubby spurs year after year—cultural facts that have been passed down to this day.

Angel-Wing Begonias enjoyed considerable popularity too, the very tall ones being grown in tubs, the smaller ones as pot plants; some, being pendant in growth, were suited to hanging baskets. Foliage varies from light apple-green to plum colour, some being spangled with silver spots and others having wavy or jagged, cut edges. Other popular begonias were the varieties with very succulent, stumpy stems and very showy large leaves. Two from this group which are still grown as porch plants are *Begonia ricinifolia maculata* with large green leaves like those of the Castor-Oil Plant *(Ricinus)* and marked underneath by conspicuous red feathery bracts, and Beefsteak Begonia *(B. erythrophylla)* with large, rounded, deep green leaves. Varieties with marbled, speckled and streaked leaves, and ones with feathery 'eyelashes' were thought very elegant and within the scope of home gardeners. Much more demanding were the tuberous begonias and rex begonias and, though grown by keen exhibitors for showing, they were mostly the province of professional gardeners with heated 'stoves' (hothouses) at their disposal.

Alongside these universal favourites (ferns, begonias, palms, etc.) a host of other plants made attractive companions. Chain of Hearts *(Ceropegia barkleyii)* was a firm favourite. With its fine trailing stems and heart-shaped purple leaves veined with silver it makes an easy hanging-basket subject; one that is not sensitive to heat or drying winds. Its very curious tubular flowers and habit of forming small tubers along the stems only add appeal. Happy in similar situations to the Chain of Hearts is the Necklace Plant *(Senecio rowleyanus)* which has perfectly round, greyish leaves on thin, trailing stems. It has white flowers, rather like miniature thistles, but they are hardly exciting. A small hanging basket overflowing with a mass of poppet-beaded stems would have delighted any child visiting a nineteenth century garden, just as they do today.

To complete a trio of succulent gems found in colonial shadehouses, we could not find a plant more suitable than the Burro's Tail Plant *(Sedum morganianum)*. Still popular today and cultivated keenly by succulent collectors and hanging-basket experts, its long stems covered with silvery-

Begonia credneri

Double tuberous begonias

grey leaves need careful attention to keep all the leaves intact, but it is worth the effort.

Completely different are the leaf-cacti, generally called Epiphyllums. Popular in the nineteenth century and still attracting collectors today, the original plants from the Caribbean and Central America were extensively hybridised by German horticulturalists. Varieties from those days are still to be found–'Deutsche Kaiserin', which is a small grower with pale pink flowers, is still very common. Modern hybrids haven't altered much since the 1880s, though colours may be more varied these days, the flowers still showing an open funnel shape with three to five rows of silky petals. These leaf-cacti can be grown in large clumps in pots or hanging baskets.

Similar in habit, with smaller flowers and round succulent stems instead of the flattened leaf form of the Epiphyllums, are the Rat's Tail Cactus (*Aporocactus flagelliformis*) with flowers in varying shades of pink, and the Mistletoe Cacti (*Rhipsalidopsis* sp.) which have tiny, waxy flowers followed by round berries.

Belonging to the same family, but much larger in every respect, is the tree-climbing Empress of the Night (*Hylocereus triangularis* syn. *H. undatus*) with its huge scented white flowers which open in the evening and close at dawn.

194   **E. & W. HACKETT,** Seedsmen, Nurserymen, &c., 73 Rundle Street, Adelaide.

FUCHSIAS.

1s. each. Our Selection 10s. per dozen.

Arabella Improved, white sepals, very large and long; well reflexed; corolla rosy pink; strong habit

Avalanche (Henderson's), very double, large and fine; sepals bright carmine, corolla dark violet plum

Beauty of Exeter, a most lovely flower; large, showy, semi-double

Beauty of Swanley, pure waxy-white sepals, elegantly reflexed; corolla bright pink

Black Prince, sepals bright carmine, large open pale pink corolla, margined deep rose

Boliviana, a very ornamental and attractive variety for outside culture; grows three to four feet high; of compact branching habit; rich crimson trumpet-shaped flowers; tube three inches in length

Bridal Bouquet, white sepals, beautiful rose-tinted corolla

Canary Bird, golden yellow foliage, prettily veined; sepals scarlet, corolla rich dark plum

Captain Boyton, fine large, double violet corolla, short tube; brilliant red, recurved sepals

Champion of the World, short tube, and broad coral red sepals well-reflexed; immense corolla, intense bright purple

Cormorant, short tube and fine large rosy crimson sepals; long semi-double bluish purple corolla

Countess of Hopetoun, double white, very fine

Creusa, rich crimson sepals, the latter short and completely reflexed, fine large corolla of a rich dark purple plum colour, shaded crimson at the base. One of the best

Crown Prince of Prussia, broad intense scarlet sepals, violet blue corolla

Duchess of Edinburgh, bright carmine sepals, well-reflexed; full double-white corolla

Earl of Beaconsfield. It produces flowers very freely in sprays three inches long; sepals light rosy carmine, corolla deep carmine

Edelweiss, a fine large flower, with full double-white corolla, rich crimson sepals, broad, long and well reflexed

Enchantress, sepals bright rose, petals broad and reflexed, large double-white corolla

Flora, short tube, large bright rosy crimson reflexed sepals, the large and full double corolla bright purple, flaked rosy carmine

Frau Emma Topfer, sepals rosy coral; corolla clear rosy blush; flowers large and double

General Roberts, a beautiful variety, of drooping habit. The flowers are 4 inches long, borne in clusters; corolla rich plum; crimson sepals

Glory, sepals very bright and completely reflexed; large violet corolla beautifully formed and widely expanded

Gracilis variegata, dwarf; leaves green, broadly margined with white

Harlequin, sepals rich carmine, broad and reflexed; very large bluish-purple corolla striped rosy pink

John Gibson, bright scarlet sepals, corolla almost black

Jubilee, very large double rose

King of the Stripes, fine bold flowers, each petal distinctly striped with red, violet-blue corolla

Little Bobby, the finest double corolla Fuchsia; rich mauve colour, scarlet sepals

Madame Jules Chretien, brilliant reddish crimson sepals, large white corolla, veined and flaked bright carmine

Miss Lucy Finniss, sepals bright coral red, corolla pure white and very double

Miss Lizzie Vidler, broad rich crimson sepals, well reflexed; large double bright violet mauve corolla

Molesworth, sepals bright carmine, well reflexed, pure white corolla, unusually large and full

Monarch, a very large flower, with bright red sepals, and rose corolla

Mr. Henry Roberts, sepals rose, well reflexed, dark crimson corolla, very broad, graceful growth

Mrs. E. G. Hill, flowers very large and double, corolla creamy white; dark red sepals, well reflexed

Mrs. Short, large double white corolla, bright rose sepals

Nouveau Mastodonte, very full and double; dark violet veined with red

Pierre Loti, enormous bluish violet double corolla, large bright red sepals

President, large flowers of good form and substance, bright vermilion sepals, corolla rich violet

Priam, short tube and broad reflexed sepals, rich crimson; corolla very double violet purple, blotched with carmine

Procumbens, small round leaves and trailing stems; excellent for hanging baskets. The flowers are orange and yellow, brownish and green, succeeded by bright red fruits

Rose of Denmark, white sepals, corolla light pink, margined with rose

Sir Garnet Wolseley, sepals bright red, well reflexed, fine double purplish violet corolla

Splendens, a Winter-flowering variety; rich crimson flowers, the ends of the sepals light green, having a peculiar Correa-like appearance

Sunray, the leaves are rich bright crimson, intermixed with white and bronzy green

Triphylla, very distinct in character; dark bronze green foliage, flowers brilliant orange scarlet

Wave of Life, beautiful golden coloured leaves, rich scarlet sepals, bright violet blue corolla

White Giant, immense flowers, very double white corolla

And other varieties.

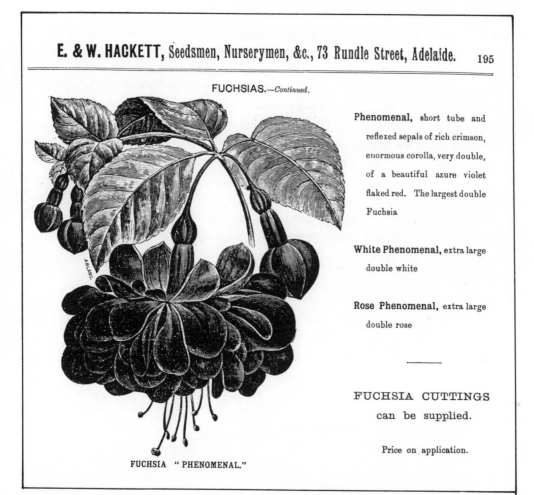

'Selected' list of fuchsias from a small nineteenth-century Adelaide nursery; doubtless bigger nurseries in the eastern states would have had even more comprehensive lists

Curiosities such as these were popular with Colonial gardeners because of their unique beauty and novelty, and because they were rare, tender and too difficult for European gardens, although they proved to be easy and tough in many parts of Australia.

Before closing this chapter, we must make mention of the fancy varieties of fuchsia which were making a big impact on shadehouse gardeners by the 1880s. We have already looked at a few of the hardy, shrubby kinds which made such attractive additions to the sheltered corners of the shrubbery, and now we will investigate the much finer varieties which inhabited the shadehouses of the times. By and large, these fuchsias were susceptible to sun, wind, dry heat and frosts, and so might be regarded as delicate in the harsh climate of much of the Antipodes. Nevertheless many a keen gardener managed somehow to obtain, and grow as pot plants in hanging baskets, at least a few of the larger flowered kinds of hybrid fuchsia.

Whatever its construction and whatever may have been grown in it, the bushhouse, shadehouse or fernery was a typical feature of the nineteenth century garden and is a vital part of any reconstruction. By its very existence, it sets the tone of a garden in period! Whether used to create a lush and overflowing garden full of interesting plants or to house a few palms and tree-ferns in a cool, shady outdoor sitting room, the bushhouse represents for many people the spirit of nineteenth century Colonial gardens.

Emerging from our shadehouse in the side garden we come into the back yard, more than likely via a vine-covered pergola, attached to the back of the house and sheltering a rainwater tank close handy to the back-door handbasin.

4 The Back Yard

The 'true' restoration or modern living with old style?

Can you cast your mind back to a back garden of your childhood? Not one of the new-fangled designer gardens of a new house in a fancy residential estate, but one of those gardens that just grew around a plain cottage on a quarter-acre block. Remember the grape vine on a trellis at the back joining up the house with the laundry, woodshed and storeroom? In pre-1900 houses, even the kitchen and bath-house were usually located near to, but separate from, the house proper and were joined to it by sheltered pathways. From the back door, a gravelled path led straight past the laundry to the clothes line—a rather ramshackle construction of galvanised wire and tall forked struts to hold the washing off the ground, which occupied an open space about halfway down the yard. Perhaps you might recall a stable and tiny horseyard, a cart shed, pigeon house and fowl house. And everyone will remember the 'little house' standing by itself down the back.

To re-create all or some of these structures would be a mighty under-taking, especially if it were done as a comprehensive exercise portraying all aspects of a Colonial home. You would need to add to our short list an underground cellar, bee hives, an airing and ironing room, a separating (or still) room for milk, a chaff and grain store for keeping animal fodder and a tack room. And there should still be room left for a generous kitchen garden—but this would be more like a museum than a home garden. I should prefer to have more garden and fewer out-buildings if I were under-taking such a task, weeding and digging being infinitely more pleasurable than railing and painting. Having now admitted that I'm no handyman, I shall set out to put you in the picture about the kitchen garden.

Firstly, the kitchen garden must be taken seriously. It was the most important part of most cottage gardens of the time as its produce frequently meant the difference between a satisfying diet and one of very meagre rations. Secondly, the vegetable patch, however large or small, must be a business-like setup, so unless you have plenty of time to put into it it is perhaps best to keep it on the small and manageable side.

The form of the back garden was usually strictly utilitarian, the area being divided by narrow footpaths into beds which could be worked conveniently from both sides. Around the perimeter and across the back, grape vines and fruit trees screened the garden and provided small luxuries for the summer table or for jam and preserves. In cooler areas a demi-wilderness of raspberries or other soft cane fruits often occupied a remote corner, while in drier areas the ground was more often uncultivated, sparsely grassed and planted with figs or almonds. More adventurous gardeners may have tried novelties such as the Prickly Pear *(Opuntia ficus-indica* or *O. tuna)* or the Tree Tomato *(Cyphomandra betacea)*. Those who kept poultry (and just about everyone did) would have kept a small patch of lucerne as green feed for the birds.

Closer to the house, on the perimeter of the intensively cultivated plots, perennial vegetables such as horseradish, rhubarb and asparagus were grown. An old tin or bucket buried up to soil level and planted with some sort of mint usually occupied some space in this part of the garden, close enough to get a good watering now and again but at a safe distance from the garden proper.

Home gardeners last century would have devoted a fair proportion of their garden space to basic commodities such as potatoes, onions, various members of the pumpkin tribe and a host of beans and peas. While antique strains of vegetables have their populists (see Joy Larkcom in *The Garden—* RHS) many gardeners today would not wish to devote much of their time to the care of such things as Blood Red Italian and Zittau Giant onions, Hair's Dwarf Mammoth peas, Magnum Bonum potatoes or the Hundred-Weight Netted pumpkin. A few things like the Turk's Turban pumpkin or the White American Custard squash could be grown for their novel appearance and their value as gourmet vegetables.

When it comes to planting the vegetable garden proper, the choice is very wide, wide enough in fact to satisfy the most fastidious vegetable gourmet. Almost any vegetable available today had its equivalent in the nineteenth century, the difference being that whereas many modern varieties are complex hybrids the rarities of yesteryear were selected seed strains.

For extensive varietal and cultural notes you could not do better than consult Henry Vilmorin's *The Vegetable Garden* (1885) which has recently been reissued in paperback. It is the classic vegetable gardening book and was written by the leading vegetable expert of the late 1800s. Herein the enthusiastic vegetable gardener will find all the good stuff about triple-trenched asparagus beds, the advantages of the different sorts of natural and chemical fertilisers and the combinations of each best suited to the edible members of the vegetable kingdom. It's not a new suggestion that the home vegetable grower should concentrate his energies on the production of early and late crops, and on varieties not usually grown by market gardeners. It is, however, sound advice by which a garden restorer can have both a faithful back garden and a productive one. Vegetable experts will need to be consulted about sowing times, harvest times and the daily operations in vegetable culture.

Among what are now popularly known as gourmet vegetables the following were available to Colonial gardeners as well as other more common vegetables: Jerusalem artichoke, asparagus bean (syn. snake bean), kale, broccoli, Chinese cabbage, Cape gooseberry, capers, cardoon (the edible thistle or artichoke), red and pink celery, celeriac, corn salad, endive, kohl rabi, leeks, cos lettuce, okra (gumbo), purple salad onions, sugar peas, parsley (flat-leaved, fern-leaved, moss-leaved, triple curled), Chinese white radish, black Spanish radish, rosella, salsify (vegetable oyster), scorzonera, sea kale, sorrel, squash, cherry tomatoes, greengage tomatoes (yellow) and pear tomatoes.

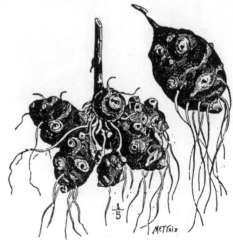

Jerusalem artichokes

White American custard squash

Vegetable marrow

Nagasaki eggplant

Duke of Albany cucumber

For the enthusiastic vegetable gardener, there is plenty of scope in a restoration scheme. Naturally, the highest standards of care, cleanliness and cultivation along with a neat and regular layout are what really make a vegetable garden, no less so now than then—not that all Colonial cottagers were neat and tidy gardeners; some plainly were not, their lack of thrift and husbandry being the subject of some concern to horticultural evangelists of last century as can be seen by this leader from *The Garden and the Field* (Tuesday, October 5, 1875. Vol. I.-No. 5).

There can be little doubt that the practice of gardening has an elevating tendency, and that the man who can take delight in tending and watching the progress of the plants under his care has a simple and innocent source of recreation not enjoyed by that one whose only pastime consists in loitering about the public-house bar, wasting precious time frittering away the money which ought to help in making his home comfortable, and putting himself in training for the Hospital or Destitute Asylum—if not for the Gaol. For this reason, therefore, we conceive that everything which will tend to the promotion of a love of gardening is worthy of support and commendation.

Some time ago, it was suggested that encouragement should be offered to the cottager and artisan class in the cultivation of small gardens, and, if we are not mistaken, the prizes offered by the S.A. Horticultural and Floricultural Society, under the head *Cottagers' Class* was the outcome of the desire. Be this as it may, we are glad to see that the classes referred to have such an opportunity afforded them, where they can compete on equal terms with each other. Of course they are still at liberty, if members of the Society, to compete with the best gardening talent that their wealthy opponents can obtain, and if they succeed in carrying off the prize all the more credit is due to them; but for general purposes it would, perhaps, be preferable if the cottagers could be induced to compete more with each other, and with this view we should be glad to

see more substantial prizes offered—and a larger number of them.

We are speaking without book in saying that the cottage gardens in the suburbs of Adelaide are almost as a rule overrun with weeds, for in a tour of many miles lately undertaken we were much pained to observe the state of neglect to which the majority of them were reduced. With so much leisure on hand it would be thought that the class referred to would have devoted some portion at least towards making their homes neat and attractive, but instead of this it is found that the greater part of them are more neglected than ever. Some appeared to have had nothing done to them for months past—beautiful and valuable plants in several places choked up with great sow-thistles run to seed, and giving promise of a large crop next year, not only on their own ground, but on that of their neighbours also; cockspur, oats, sheepweed, and everything noxious left in full luxuriance, fences all awry and broken down; gates wide open, and in some places no gates; hedges neglected, painting neglected—everything neglected.

There are a few exceptions, where the gardens are as neat as could be desired, but the above is a true picture of by far too many of the cottage gardens; and it is with the hope and desire of an alteration for the better that we revive the suggestion that prizes should offered for the neatest garden, and the prize-list more generally extended in the Cottagers' Class.

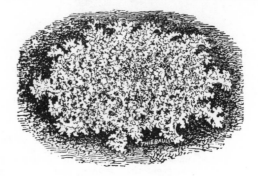

White curled endive

Very long pure white vegetable marrow

The Currant Tomato.—This is very ornamental when grown in pots. It requires exactly the same treatment as other kinds of the

The Currant Tomato.

Tomato. The seed should be sown at once in a warm house or frame. When large enough the seedlings should be potted off singly into small pots, and shifted on as becomes necessary. The best soil is turfy loam, with enough sand added to make it porous. Too much wood should not be allowed ; and those shoots which remain should, when sufficient fruit is set on them, be stopped by pinching out their growing points. When the fruit is swelling occasional doses of liquid-manure will be of benefit. This Tomato may be used for culinary purposes, and it is especially suitable for pickles.

Building a Summer-house.—I have built a very pretty rustic summer-house in this way : Mark out an octagon, each side 4 ft. long ; plant at each corner a rough straight pole 4 in. thick and 9 ft. long. Char or double tar 3 ft. of the thickest end and put 2 ft. in the ground. Level the tops, and connect them all round with crosspieces of similar timber, a few inches of each end sticking out. Take another piece 3 ft. long and saw one end to a point ; from it, as a centre, nail all round it, like spokes in a wheel, eight straight clothes-props slanting down at an angle of 40.° Put this on the top of the upright poles, and nail each loose prop end to the top of a pole, letting 6 in. or 12 in. extend beyond. This makes the roof. Now fill up with rustic lattice-work (1 in. or 2 in. thick) eight of the sides, leaving one for the entrance : then lattice the roof, or, better still, thatch it. Use strong French nails and the gimlet when

A Home-made Summer-house.

necessary. Fix the crosspieces into the tops of the poles by boring with a centre-bit through the whole, and hammer in an iron peg, 6 in. long. Leave the bark on the wood, which may be sized and varnished. Use throughout the hardest wood possible ; Oak or Beech for the poles, and Beech or Hazel for the lattice. Plant a good climber, for instance, scented Clematis, C. Jackmanni, Wistaria, Ampelopsis, Veitchi, scented Jasmine, Honeysuckle, climbing Rose, against each pole ; well fill the outside borders with hardy Ferns. In two years you have a floral paradise. My house cost me under £1 without the thatch, but I did all the work myself.—W. L.

Two items from a *Gardening Illustrated* magazine of 1880

Maybe you won't want to go all the way with the restoration of your back garden; if a *potager* is not for you, you will be in good company—at least a hundred year's worth of fellow-travellers! No need to abandon your garden restoration project though, for a much simplified arrangement can be developed which reflects cottage garden style, but involving much less labour. This approach is particularly attractive for owners of cottages which are not permanently occupied. It is equally applicable to villa gardens, combining formal elements with plants which can be managed formally or informally. The general idea is to create the formal layout by setting out a rectangular grid of beds and pathways, which for ease of maintenance would be wide enough to let a lawnmower pass, and to line the bed edges with a permanent border of agapanthus (I prefer the miniature form) or belladonnas. Once these have been established a few years, they will fill out into hedges of foliage. The beds should be large enough to have a good clear space in the middle when the edging plants have grown.

Beds at least two metres by two and a half would be about right. In the centre of each bed could be planted cottage garden shrubs such as honeysuckle, lilacs, forsythia, *Hibiscus syriacus*, old-fashioned shrub roses, mock orange, Chinese Beauty Bush *(Kolkwitzia)*, St John's Wort *(Hypericum)*, weigela or some other old favourites. These should be allowed to grow naturally with little trimming. An underplanting of tough, colourful South African bulbs would make a colourful spring carpet and need no care other than a quick tidy-up with an electric nylon-cord weed trimmer in late October. With a little extra work at the outset putting a barrier about twenty centimetres deep into the soil inside the edging of agapanthus, all the hassles of annual root pruning can be avoided. Similar simple beds could be set out with lavender, rosemary, or Lavender Cotton *(Santolina pectinata)* as the edging, or even used to create whole blocks of foliage, but these require more attention and trimming. If you've got the time and inclination the effects of the more varied planting could be striking. Within such a formal framework a serene composition of greys could be built up using lavenders, santolina, Wormwood *(Artemisia)* and common sage with a filling of lamb's tongue, silver-leaved gazania, *Cerastium tomentosum, Veronica cineraria, Sedum spectabile, Artemisia stelleriana, Iris florentina, Thymus languinosus, Dianthus* spp., *Senecio cineraria,* gypsophila, *Convolvulus cneorum, Onopordon acanthium, Verbascum olympicum,* Rose Campion *(Lychnis coronaria), Chrysanthemum haradjanii, Senecio maritima* or *Ruta graveolens.* Such a setting would be the one place where I would avoid the usual conglomeration of plants found in a cottage garden. I should prefer to use only one or two plants in each bed, say spikey *Iris florentina* with trailing *Artemisia stelleriana* or *Stachys lanata* with *Chrysanthemum haradjanii*. This idea would be a real feature if some of the shrubs were displaced by a regular pattern of standard roses. Such formalism would suit the altogether grander style of a villa garden better than a simple cottage and could be supplemented with a simple arrangement of big tubs to heighten the Mediterranean feeling of a villa garden. Again, such a garden is both more labour-intensive and suited to a town garden than the original concept, though still retaining the nineteenth century feeling.

My choice of roses for this garden would be 'Lady Hillingdon', 'Buff Beauty', 'Perle d'Or', 'Souvenir de Mme Boullett' and 'Crepuscule'—all lovely old-gold colours—but you could be happier with pinks such as 'Mme Lambard', 'Monsieur Tillier', 'Souvenir d'Un Ami', 'Papa Gontier', 'Mme Charles' and 'Noella Nabonand'.

We seem to have come a long way from the vegetable garden, if not the back yard, so while we are this far afield from a vegetable patch in the nineteenth century we might as well take a look at the effects of modern life on the back yard.

In a more affluent and leisured society with few pressing needs to grow enough to feed ourselves the back yard, more than other parts of the garden, has changed its role quite radically. Instead of chicken runs, out-houses, wells and stables, you are far more likely to find basketball hoops, barbecues, patios and swimming pools—the problem is to meld these into the overall Colonial feel of the place. Fortunately all that goes before—the front garden and the side gardens—has served to create the impression of a cottage or villa garden so a slight deception may find acceptance in the modern eye. The important thing is to continue the impression by the use of a suitable variety of plants arrayed in similar fashion to what has gone before, and to admit the modern intrusions without trying to hide them. If it is possible to plan the features before the garden is made, I should advise the use of simple formal shapes for swimming pools and paving areas. The hard edges can easily be softened by a profusion of overflowing plants, but the basic shapes of square, rectangle and circle are always in keeping. The kidney-shaped swimming pool and free-form paving areas are strictly modern concepts and no matter how they are planted they always look wrong in a nineteenth century garden. If you find your newly purchased garden blessed with such ill-fitting structures, then, unless you are very wealthy, you are stuck with them. If, on the other hand, you contemplate building such things, then choose simple formal shapes every time and eschew modern curlicues and staccato angles.

Should you attempt to disguise these free-form modernistic features? I should say 'No'. Old-fashioned additions to modern structures generally don't do anything to blend them in. Instead, the violent contrasts between, say, a modern brick barbecue and an old-style gazebo only serve to heighten the sense of alienation. The best course would be simply to tie the whole outdoor living area together with lawn or paving and screen it from the rest of the garden by some sort of light fencing, preferably well clothed with climbers and shrubs—old-fashioned ones, of course! A semi-hedge made this way should be about two metres high. Useful plants for such a screen are any of the jasmines or clematis such as *C. cirrhosa* 'Balaerica', *C. napaulensis, C. tangutica, C. viticella* or *C. flammula.* Some of the newly introduced honeysuckles would be well suited too—especially *Lonicera hildebrandiana* with its large ever-green leaves and golden flowers, and *L. serotina* cv. 'Magnifica' with silver-grey leaves and brilliant orange-scarlet tabular flowers. I would avoid anything that is really vigorous as you wouldn't want to end up with an overgrown eyesore.

Useful light shrubs for such a project would be *Cedronella triphylla, Salvia rutilans* (Pineapple Sage), or scented-leaf pelargoniums such as *P. graveolens, P.* × 'Lady Plymouth', *P.* × 'Mabel Gray', *P. papillionaceum* and *P. vitifolium.*

If space permits, and you have the energy, a simple structure of upright rustic logs spaced two and a half to three and a half metres apart and about the same height, linked at the top by very loosely strung wire or heavy rope, could increase the amount of screening, give visual interest and add to the nineteenth century feeling of a secret garden once vines and climbers had been trained over it. On such a structure, planting should still be light—it's the impression of *separateness* created by the structure and planting that is wanted, not a heavy planting which completely hides the area. Perhaps one or two more substantial climbers could be admitted, but only one or two!

Three less commonly found climbers which I would prefer over the more obvious choices of Glory Vine, Lady Banks rose and Rambler roses are *Vitis coignetiae* with huge round leaves and brilliant purple-red autumn colours, the rose 'Mme Gregoire Staechelin' with masses of blowsy two-tone pink flowers and *Wistaria sinensis alba* or the double blue form. All these are variations on the more obvious choices but sufficiently distinct to impart that feeling of richness and diversity which touched the old cottage and villa gardens.

If a little terrace house is being restored, almost the whole of the back garden would be occupied by outdoor living areas and garaging, so cottage garden colour would be limited to a changing display of annuals in large tubs. The tubs could be permanently planted with your special favourites—a rose or camellia, say. High boundary walls need some veil of greenery and flowers but nothing that will become a pest or a chore. For sunny walls, I would use climbers of moderate habits such as the large-flowered clematis, jasmine or maybe a rose—'Paul's Scarlet Climber' or 'Sombreuil' would be about right for size. For shaded walls, the choice could be Trachelospermum or one of the very slow ivies—*Hedera canariensis albo-maculata* (white leaves speckled green) or *H. helix deltoidea* with leaves like arrowheads—the Climbing Hydrangea *(Hydrangea petiolaris)* or even the exquisite Chilean Waxflower *(Lapageria rosea)* if you can get one! Room being at a premium, the choice of the one or two trees that might be fitted in must be limited to those that give at least two tangible pleasures and let in the sun in the winter. *Magnolia salicifolia* with lemon-scented starry white flowers and taller growth than *M. stellata* could be a possibility. *Paulownia imperialis* with blue jacaranda-type flowers and round furry leaves might be another. The first is slow growing and the last can be pollarded (cut right back to the trunks) if necessary. Of course, you might wish to indulge in the pleasures of a walnut, pecan or fruit tree, any of which would be acceptable and attractive.

In small gardens such as these it's very difficult to recreate accurately a cottage garden. The right atmosphere can be created by the careful choice of plants, construction materials and fittings. The same applies to those whose back gardens must accommodate the activities of a young family. The feeling of cottage-garden cosiness can be brought about by an awareness of the basic essentials: variety and profusion and a maximum of informality within a regularised setting.

Shelter belt of pines and a massive hedge of Lamberts cypress, 'Buda', Castlemaine, Vic.

A Garden of Whimsy—the Shell Garden, Millicent, SA

A Faithful Friend, Gisborne, Vic.

California Poppies *(Eschscholzia)* with *Gladiolus colvillei* 'The Bride' and Silver Groundsel *(Centaurea ragusina).*

Garden Urn, Moonee Ponds, Vic.

Agapanthus orientalis aureo-vittatus—the golden variegated agapanthus with a small *Agave americana medio-picta* in an old pot.

5 On the Verandah

Potted plants

Having already passed through the fernery of our mind's eye's restoration, we should return briefly to the front verandah to take in the collection of potted plants displayed there. Keen gardeners last century were no less acquisitive than their modern-day counterparts. Delicate plants were sheltered from the harsh elements in the shadehouse, small glasshouses or frames. Hardier specimens were housed, much as they are today, in places safe from the sun's scorching rays, but where the free flow of air and intensity of light were sufficient to keep growth healthy and compact. The shelter provided by the overhang of a front verandah provided an almost ideal place for growing hardy pot plants.

The first of these might be small palms, frequently a Kentia palm, Rhapis or Cycad, but just as likely a camellia or two in halved wine-barrels, half of a forty-four gallon drum or a square kerosene tin (suitably painted, of course). In the drier areas, hydrangeas were very popular as porch plants because by using imported mountain soil or chemical means the growing mix could be made acid enough to produce blue flowers—desired so much more than the common pinks produced in the inland plains and alkaline soil areas.

Other subjects for big tubs were cliveas, pink Tiger Lilies *(L. speciosum)*, the common orange Tiger Lily *(L. tigrinum)*, the Sacred Lily of the Incas *(Ismene festalis)* or the Eucharist Lily *(Eurycles amazonica)*. Hippeastrums, too, were enjoying their first big vogue and were available in red and white and striped combinations of these two colours, only the refinements of the blooms separating them from the majestic blooms of today. German hybridisers were the main workers with these bulbs, possibly because of the concentration of German explorers and botanists in their South American homelands.

In the really dry areas in the days before regular water supply systems were installed, such drought-hardy bulbs were valued pot plants as they could be kept going with waste water from kitchen and bathroom without damage. Even today, there are many who swear by the drainings and dregs of the teapot—a demonstration of the staying power of this lore of Colonial gardeners.

In an earlier chapter, 'florists' flowers' were mentioned in passing as being not much used by cottage and villa gardeners as they required too much attention when grown as cool glasshouse subjects, what with damping down, ventilating and pest control to be attended to daily, as well as watering, feeding, pruning and tying up of each potted plant. But where growing by the dozen was entirely too much to manage, growing one or two specimens to perfection was a challenge.

Calceolaria hybrida

Among the most popular florists' flowers were calceolarias (Purse Flowers), cinerarias, cyclamen, schizanthus (Poor Man's Orchid) and salpiglossis. 'Florists', in case I haven't made it obvious, were not flower sellers and providers of wreaths and floral gifts as we know them today, but a class of gardening enthusiasts who specialised in collecting, breeding, growing and showing a restricted group of plants selected for their floral perfection according to the ideals of the day. Those ideals, put very generally, were flowers circular in outline, with clear and regular markings—stripes, edges, flakes, spots, eye-zones, etc.—and a uniform arrangement of petals. Amateur and professional gardeners have delighted in this solitary recreation since at least the eighteenth century.

Cineraria hybrida grandiflora

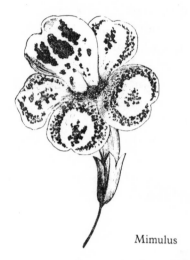

Mimulus

Salpiglossis variabilis grandiflora

Plants which have attracted florists at various times since then have been auriculas, pinks, tulips, ranunculus, anemone, camellia, pansies, violas, hyacinths, dahlias, roses and chrysanthemums, as well as those previously mentioned, and others too (see Roy Gender's *The Cottage Garden and Old-Fashioned Flowers*, Pelham, 1983).

It's not hard to see how these basic ideals of perfection have influenced flowers and flower shows right up to the present. Contemporary developments in paeonies, day lilies *(Hemerocallis)*, gladiolus, iris, liliums and roses all show the strong influence of the 'round and regular' school of thought. Fortunately for today's gardeners there are some breeders sufficiently individualistic to persist in raising and introducing plants with a greater degree of variety than the old florists' rules would allow us. We would be foolish to throw away the plants that have come down to us from the florists of old, but neither should we let them dominate a garden restoration.

Other flowering small plants commonly found on the verandah were ordinary garden things chosen for the pleasures of close association—the colour and perfume of favourite flowers brought almost indoors. Freesias, lachenalias, geraniums, campernellas *(Narcissus campernella)*, Regal pelargoniums and various primulas are just a few of the everyday plants put into pots and brought onto the verandah.

Far less common, and most intriguing, were the varied assortments of succulent plants cultivated by many householders. All sorts of cacti and other succulents were grown in everything from half wine-barrels to jam tins. The 'cute' use of old boots as pots seems to have been a development of the 1950s, and perhaps this novel idea should be eschewed. If you are seeking to develop some sense of Colonial rusticity perhaps you could use one or two old cast iron cooking pots as plant containers—if you could keep them out of the hands of the antique collectors!

Exotic specimens from South Africa, South America, the dry lands of Central America and the western United States were imported as mature field-collected plants in the days before Commonwealth quarantine laws. Seed-raising played its part too, as well as propagation by offsets, and succulent plants gained a wide popularity. Aside from their desirability as potted plants, many succulents were advertised as being very useful for edging and bedding-out. The most popular plants for these purposes were some of the rosette-forming succulents known as Echeverias. Ranging from ten to thirty centimetres in diameter, these hardy Mexicans made colours such as silver, pink and olive-green available for permanent plantings in garden colour schemes. The following are among the hardiest and most prolific: *Echeveria elegans*, silver foliage; *E. albicans*, white foliage; *E. metallica*, metallic grey foliage; *E.* × 'Huth's Pink', rose pink foliage; *E.* × 'Perle von Nurenberg', pink with purple edge; *E. gilva*, olive-green foliage; *E. byrnesii*, bright green foliage; *E. secunda*, pointed silver leaves.

All are frost tender and suffer badly in hailstorms. A single row of rosettes lined out in early spring will soon multiply into a solid edging that's proof against the hottest summer. Should you be blessed with a drystone wall (one with no cement between the stones) a few Echeveria rosettes tucked into the crevices here and there will soon settle in and look as if they've been there for at least one hundred years!

If you haven't such a wall, then the Echeverias will look just as well in an array of squat pots on your verandah, multiplying happily while they wait for you to build them a wall for a home! By the way, drystone walling is a most appropriate way to build terrace walls and low retaining walls in Colonial gardens; you have only to look at some of the fine examples of such walling in the Blue Mountains, the Dandenongs and in Tasmania to see how well it looks and to realise its significance in Colonial construction techniques.

We will get back to pot plants in a moment but let's quickly look at how to build a drystone wall. First you need a reason to build one—to make a terrace or retaining wall is usually it. Secondly, you need a strong back, an ample supply of patience and at least one willing worker! The largest stones

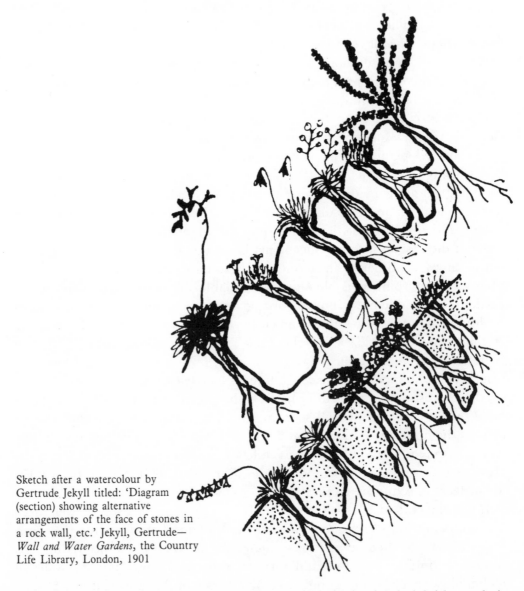

Sketch after a watercolour by
Gertrude Jekyll titled: 'Diagram
(section) showing alternative
arrangements of the face of stones in
a rock wall, etc.' Jekyll, Gertrude—
Wall and Water Gardens, the Country
Life Library, London, 1901

will be needed for the bottom course and should be buried laid on their
largest faces, with a slight slope backwards from the open face of the wall.
Packing the soil carefully behind and between the rocks as each course is laid,
the work will be accomplished slowly but with a feeling of satisfaction for the
workers. It is possible to plant such a wall with thymes, campanulas and
small succulents as you go but deft footwork is required to avoid crushing the
small plants as the stones for the higher courses are carried over them. Not
an easy feat when heavy stones are being lumped about.

Now let us get back to the succulent pot plants. In large tubs such familiars as aloes, agaves and yuccas would be most suitable, but which ones are appropriate choices out of the dozens available? Knowing the pleasure Colonial gardeners took in unusual forms, you could choose from these curiosities:

Aloe plicatilus (the Fan Aloe) Slowly makes a multiple-branched bush with a stout grey trunk. Small spikes of tubular orange flowers appear in late winter;

Agave americana medio-picta (the Century Plant) Grey-green edges with a broad golden central band;

Agave americana striata (another form of the Century Plant) This one has the entire leaf surface flecked with intermittent fine yellow stripes;

Agave victoriae-reginae, a stout-leaved plant with conspicuous white markings on the leaves. A very formal looking plant. Similar are *A. fernandi-regis, A. parviflora* and *A. filifera*. Other outstanding Agaves are *A. parrasana, A. potatorum verschaffeltii* and *A. stricta*.

Yucca gloriosa va. *medio-picta*, a broad leaved plant about one metre across with stiff grey leaves coloured with a bright gold central stripe. It flowers well with the usual tall spikes of cream bells;

Yucca glauca va. *striata* "Tricolor", a striking plant with very narrow leaves heavily margined with cream. In cold weather and during the growing season the leaf edges are coloured pink. Rarely flowers;

Yucca recurvifolia va. *marginata*, recurving leaves with a wide margin of yellow, makes a most attractive fountain of foliage. Flowers well and produces a good supply of offsets.

For smaller pots, the range of succulent plants becomes much larger. Aloes such as the Partridge-breasted Aloe *(A. variegata)* and *A. aristata* were well known, along with aeoniums, pig-face (mesembryanthemums), crassulas, *Portulacaria* (Jade Plant) and especially sempervivums, the House Leeks. Popular since the Middle Ages for their reputation as protectors of houses against thunderbolts, these tiny rosetted plants were given a fresh boost by the activities of alpinists during the Victorian era, and many outstanding varieties were introduced at that time. They are ideal subjects for pots, being hardy, colourful and prolific multipliers. There are at least a hundred varieties in the hands of private collectors, a few of the best being *Sempervivum arachnoideum* and the varieties 'Malby Hybrid', 'Sir William Lawrence', 'Triste', 'Olivette', 'Omicron', 'Cleveland Morgan', 'Old Copper', 'Flamingo', 'Grigg's Surprise', 'Ohio Burgundy', 'Raspberry Ice', 'Jungle Shadows' and 'Blue Moon'.

These are not all nineteenth century varieties, but it's very hard to determine just what varieties were grown then, so great is the confusion of species, cultivars and hybrids.

A group of cacti

Sempervivums are natives of Europe and quite naturally were objects of sentimental attachment for many settlers, but the gardeners of the period were equally enthusiastic about the latest succulent novelties from South Africa. Haworthias were one such group that found early favour as attractive pot plants. There are two distinct groups in this family; one section has green succulent leaves with "see-through" tips and the other section has grey-green leaves with pearly white spots. A visit to the garden of any succulent collector would almost certainly enable you to obtain a few specimens.

During the nineteenth century the flow of plants from the New World to Europe included many cacti. As pot plants they were especially attractive because of their unique form and often brilliant flowers. As in many other plant families, the cactus tribe is still the subject of much name changing and revision by botanists, so making a comprehensive list could easily turn into a nightmare. I will list a few that should be recognised by the cactus buff, even if they do preface their sales with the comment, "Of course, you know the name's been changed to...!" For pot culture the Mammillarias are both easy and very pretty, Rebutias and Echinopsis too. For a big impact the Golden Ball Cactus *(Echinocactus grusonii)* can't be beaten, though the Ferocactus, heavily armed with hooked thorns in black, red or tan, are almost as stunning. The Peanut Cactus *(Chamaecereus silvestrii)* is an old familiar well suited to pot culture. Its cheery tomato-red blooms are produced in profusion on a no-fuss plant. These few are but a small number from an amazing procession of succulent plants which first came to our gardens last century. The few that have been mentioned are not especially significant, they're just a sample of the range of plants available to Colonial gardeners for use as front verandah pot plants.

Before closing this chapter on pot plants, we should take a look at the pots themselves. Passing mention has already been made of half wine-barrels, half forty-four gallon drums and jam tins which, though not always aesthetically pleasing, did serve their purpose well and demonstrate the commonsense approach of most Colonial gardeners. There were real pots too, beautiful terracotta pots with rolled round rims and bands of herring-bone decoration. They came in all sizes from tiny 2.5 centimetre thumb pots right up to huge palm pots. There were special purpose pots too. Seed pans were shallow and wide mouthed; orchid pots had deep slits incised into the sides and often had holes pierced just below the rim to facilitate hanging. Some were even made with a flat surface so they could be hung against a wall. 'Long Toms' were very tall in comparison to the pots made to accommodate shallow, fibrous rooted plants such as azaleas and tuberous begonias.

Pots such as these are still made by a few potteries, though not usually in continuous runs. Production is frequently limited to only one or two lots each year as they are hand thrown and the decoration applied by hand as well. All this means that the pots cost more than the usual machine-made clay pots.

If cost is an important consideration in the purchase of the dozen or so pots you may need then you could look to the purchase of seconds-quality pots. These have minor imperfections, usually hair-line cracks. From careful inspection you should be able to gauge the extent of the imperfection and the likely lifespan of the pot. Some variety in the pots chosen for display on the front verandah can be achieved by introducing one or two jardinieres of Oriental or European design, but restraint should be exercised less the cottage porch be furnished in a manner too opulent and exotic! Some further variety could be added by using home-made pots constructed from hollow logs cut to convenient lengths and with one end closed over with a sheet of perforated tin or wire mesh. A mixture of a few precious decorative pots, some clay pots and some home-made improvisations would be entirely appropriate housing for a collection of potted plants on a cottage verandah.

6 Covering the Woodshed

Climbers

With the number of sheds and out-buildings in the back yard of a Colonial home, something must have driven the home gardener to the effort of establishing creepers and climbers over them.

In many instances the planting of vines was a practical solution to several problems; how to keep those corrugated iron buildings cool; how to use the wall space to grow vine crops and how to cover up buildings that in most cases were strictly utilitarian and basic in appearance and finish. Being such a long-lasting material, and one that was widely available and new, corrugated iron is the most commonly-met building material in old gardens. Even where buildings were made from solid timber slabs or mortar and rubble construction, they were quite often covered over with the newer tin sheets to hide salt damp or simply to 'modernise' their appearance. But still the walls had to be covered—and so they were, not only with tin but also with climbers.

For big sheds such as cart sheds (or in modern times carports and garages), there were some really vigorous climbers that could be relied on to smother the biggest shed in a few short years. Among them were several plants with strong sentimental appeal. The Lady Banks rose is one big climber that is frequently seen on old buildings. The double yellow form is the most common, but there is a double white which flowers just as well and has the added bonus of a fine violet-scented perfume. There are also single yellow and white forms which would turn the topic of many a conversation. Heavier foliage and larger double white blooms are found on *Rosa* × *fortuneana* which was popular last century as a climber and as an understock for budding roses. (It is still used for this purpose to produce rose bushes for areas with extremely sandy soils.) Unlike the light green foliage of the Lady Banks roses, *R.* × *fortuneana* has very dark green leaves which are a perfect foil for the white flowers.

The wistaria is another cover-all that really grew in popularity during the nineteenth century. Apart from the usual lilac form *(Wistaria floribunda)*, other cultivars were collected from gardens in China and introduced in Europe—the white, pink and double blue forms. If you want to plant a wistaria why not try to get one of these less common varieties? You may have to search around a bit to get one but the result after a few year's growth would be a specimen plant that would have appealed to any keen gardener during the reign of Queen Victoria. China was not the only place to give wistarias to the plant collector; from Japan came *W. multijuga* with flowering stems well over a metre in length—sufficiently impressive to satisfy even the most particular gardener. Also from Japan came *Akebia trifoliata*, a vigorous

Wistaria-covered pergola

Akebia

twining plant with graceful leaves resembling a clover-leaf. In late spring, masses of smoky maroon-purple 'bobble' flowers, giving off a light but far-reaching perfume.

More spectacular in foliage, though without any blossom to speak of, are the true vines, the Vitis family. We can all call to mind, no doubt, hoary old specimens of the Crimson Glory Vine (*Vitis* × 'Ganzin Glory') with massive gnarled butts and arm-thick branches spreading far and wide. Recently published research proposes the name 'Ganzin Glory' for a vine commonly grown in Southern Australia under a variety of invalid and confused names. It has been sold as 'Glory Vine', 'Crimson Glory Vine', 'Alicante Bouchet', 'Teinturier' and 'Teinturier Male' (See A.J. Antcliffe, 'The Glory Vine of South Australia', *Adelaide Botanical Gardens Journal* 2 (4), pp.353–354, 1980.)

There were fruiting grapes too, for the table, jam-making and drying. And there was one other, less often seen, that should be grown far more widely— *Vitis coignetiae*, introduced in 1875 from Japan to Europe and thence to the colonies. It grows strongly and has leaves which are rounder and less pointed than the usual grape varieties. They are a curious bright green with a bronzy overtone and a very distinct network of veins covering the surface. The undersides are thick with a light rusty-coloured felt. Quite different, and made more outstanding by their dinner-plate size. If all this is not enough it ends its season with an autumn display of vivid orange, scarlet and purple colours, far superior to its more suburban cousins. For all this it is not often seen. A few old-timers exist, and even though it has a reputation for being hard to strike from cuttings it's not so hard as to explain its scarcity. If you have a shed that needs covering get one; you won't be disappointed!

Before leaving Asia for southern climes and some other strong climbers, let's look at *Jasminum polyanthum*, so common these days it's almost ho-hum, and yet it's anything but that. Despite its covering power the fine foliage and delicate, graceful sprays of bloom lighten the dark green growth so that the effect is not overbearing.

Two rampant creepers from the south introduced to Europe as fine-flowered glass-house plants were the Trumpet Vines, once known as *Bignonia* but now split off by botanists into a legion of relatives and leaving *Bignonia* almost bereft of family—in fact only two remain. Gardeners in Australia found only the frost deterred their rampaging growth. Possibly the most stunning of them is *Campsis radicans* from the south-east United States, which has flowers similar in shape to a gloxinia, brick-red with an orange throat.

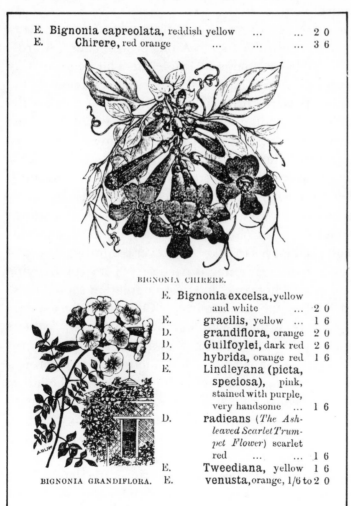

E. **Bignonia capreolata,** reddish yellow 2 0
E. **Chirere,** red orange 3 6

BIGNONIA CHIRERE.

E.	**Bignonia excelsa,** yellow and white ...	2 0
E.	**gracilis,** yellow ...	1 6
D.	**grandiflora,** orange	2 0
D.	**Guilfoylei,** dark red	2 6
D.	**hybrida,** orange red	1 6
E.	**Lindleyana (picta, speciosa),** pink, stained with purple, very handsome ...	1 6
D.	**radicans** (*The Ash-leaved Scarlet Trumpet Flower*) scarlet red	1 6
E.	**Tweediana,** yellow	1 6
E.	**venusta,** orange, 1/6 to	2 0

BIGNONIA GRANDIFLORA.

A list of bignonias available from a nineteenth-century nursery

Such brilliant flowers teamed with lush, dark green leaves and supreme vigour added a touch of tropical luxuriance to many a shed and fence. The other ramper is *Pandorea ricasoliana* with leaves and flowers similar but for their colouring, which is pale pink with deeper veining leading to a rose-pink patch in the throat of each flowery trumpet. Each is strong enough to cover a cow-shed, and the cow too if she stood still for only a week or two! Another member of the family Bignoniaceae, *Tecomaria capensis* from South Africa, is only slightly less vigorous, though it seems to have been used more as a hedge than a climber. It has metallic green foliage arranged in leaflets of 7–11 and strident orange-red tubular flowers in small clusters. All three are determined 'doers' with a considerable degree of willfulness. Be cautioned! Only the bravest should plant them; prune ruthlessly or the entire garden will be the subject of a botanical coup d'etat!

The climbing fig, *Ficus repens*, is a very strong grower but has too many disadvantages to be considered desirable today. All its growth goes upwards, leaving only a mass of tangled bare stems at eye-level. The delicate, tiny leaves of young plants soon give way to larger, gross, leathery versions as the plant matures. It has neither flowers nor fruits to recommend it and has the particularly thuggish habit of strangling anything within reach of its stems. The only way to control the climbing fig is by hard trimming with hedge clippers in mid-summer and early autumn. For my mind too much work for so few returns. Equally vigorous, and still a strangler, given half the chance, is the Algerian ivy *(Hedera canariensis)* and its varieties, 'Gloire de Marengo', the common large-leaved variegated ivy, and 'Striata', the dark green form with a golden central blotch. Unlike *Ficus repens* these ivies have sufficient appeal in their brightly coloured leaves to make whatever trimming is needed worthwhile. But do remember that trimming is necessary. Can you imagine your disgust at the slow death of a host tree due to strangulation should these great groundcovers get started up the trunks of trees? Or what of the expense involved should stems get under the eaves and inside the roof of your expensively restored villa, lifting the cladding and admitting possums, starlings and sparrows? Better perhaps to choose something less vigorous.

I have no figs to offer but one ivy stands out as a look-alike for the larger *Hedera canariensis*, though it is less robust. It is *Hedera colchica* 'Dentata Variegata' with large leaves broadly banded outside with creamy gold.

Strong growers but definitely not in the massive class are *Clematis montana* (white), *C. montana rubens* (pink) and *C. chrysocoma* (pearly-white). They are all magnificent performers and have been known since the late 1800s. Personally I dislike the pink of *C. montana rubens*, finding the colour too murky and too mauve. But the white form *(C. montana)* is pure and pristine, and almost a must for covering a small shed or wall. *Clematis armandii* just scrapes in, being introduced in 1900, but it is such a splendid plant that I would not have left it out even if it had been introduced in 1910 (and you will find there are several others like this that are too good to leave out and have been included because they are characteristic of the age even if not quite chronologically correct). At any season the foliage of *C. armandii* is a knockout: deep bronzy fingers up to 18cm long which slowly deepen to a glossy rich green as they age. The new growth is almost red. In early spring or late winter it smothers itself with tumbling tresses of perfumed white flowers. Magnificent yet still cottagey. It's an evergreen too, so would be perfect to cover an ugly shed. Like all clematis it must have shade and cool at the roots. Either protect the roots with other low plants to create shade or use straw spread thickly to make a mulch. I like using straw myself as when bought by the bale it is easy to handle and convenient. When the binding twine is cut the bales fall apart in handy, compressed wads ready to spread. It doesn't smell either. After a short time in the weather the pale yellow straw turns grey and is hardly noticeable. It will only last one season but by the following year your foundation planting of lavenders, scented-leaf geraniums, etc., will be established and create the shade at the roots which clematis must have.

When thinking of cottage gardens and clematis most people would conjure up visions of the large-flowered sorts. These began to appear in England and France in the 1850s, and in the next twenty years an extraordinary spate of breeding created the style of bloom still held up as the ideal of perfection today. Obtaining plants can be a problem. Nurserymen seem to have more bad years than good when it comes to propagating them; yet it all seems so easy in Christopher Lloyd's very readable monograph *Clematis* (Collins, London, 1965) so maybe his advice needs some local interpretation. The outcome of all this is that gardeners can't always get the clematis they want and so snap up whichever are available. At least as far as appearance goes there is precious little difference between nineteenth and twentieth century cultivars. Genuine nineteenth century varieties include 'W.E. Gladstone'— large silky lavender flowers with darker stamens (1881); 'Mrs Hope'—huge satin-finished light blue flowers with overlapping petals (1875); 'Durandii' —brilliant dark blue flowers with pale stamens, not a climber but a scrambler; great planted with apricot shrub roses such as 'Perle d'Or' or 'Buff Beauty' (1870); 'Duchess of Edinburgh'—double, greenish-white flowers (1876); 'Belle of Woking'—double French-grey (silvery-white);

'Lady Londesborough'—silver-grey single blooms (1869); 'Fair Rosamond'—scented blush white (1873); 'Henryi'—large white with dark stamens (1855); 'Ville de Lyon'—brilliant beetrooty-red, bright but not garish (1899); 'Star of India'—reddish-purple, starry petals (1867); 'Gypsy Queen'—very dark purple-red, starry petals (1877); 'Sir Garnet Wolseley'—deep lavender (1880); 'Miss Crawshay'—mauve-pink, early blooms, double (1873); 'Comtesse de Bouchaud'—pink, vigorous and very prolific (1900); 'Nelly Moser'—almost white with a deeper pinkish bar in the centre of each petal (1897).

There are others too, but as I said most people are happy to take whatever they can get, and any of them will look right in a colonial garden. For pruning instructions I suggest you read Christopher Lloyd. His book *Clematis* (see 'Recommended Reading') is the last word on this and other clematis matters.

Clematis viticella, C. flammula, C. alpina, C. × 'Venosa Violacea' and *C. campaniflora* are also good small climbers with small flowers which are in period and available from time to time. They are easily raised from seed though they sometimes take their time about it (1–2 years) and the Royal Horticultural Society seed list usually contains several species. *Clematis tangutica*, the Lemon Peel Clematis (1898) and its similar cousin *C. orientalis* (1731) are two curious types with small flowers which have 'thick-skinned' petals in clear yellow and greenish-yellow.

Colonial gardeners in Australia and New Zealand also had some native species of clematis—Old Man's Beard, Traveller's Joy or Virgin's Bower they were called. *Clematis aristata* from Australia is a common bushland climber and it was brought early into settlers' gardens because of its similarities to the Old Man's Beard *(C. vitalba)* of the homelands, and for its perfumed flowers. *Clematis afoliata, C. forsteri, C. hookerana, C. parviflora* and *C. paniculata* are all New Zealand species which attracted the attention of garden-conscious settlers. Though frequently referred to as 'old favourites' for sheltered walls, *C. napaulensis* and *C. cirrhosa* va. *balearica* are two whose dates of introduction elude me. I would include them anyhow, for their winter flowers are small and charming. Each bears pendant flowers of greenish-yellow. The first has protruding anthers of clear lavender and the latter has maroon flecks on the petals. Neither are world-shattering, not yet great rarities, but both are welcome and just the sort of 'vegetable curiosity' so loved last century. *Clematis napaulensis* is deciduous from late summer until winter and *C. cirrhosa* va. *balearica* is evergreen with dark bronzy fern-like leaves.

A rare pale pink form of Pride of Madeira *(Echeium fastuosum)*

Leucojum aestivum—Snowflakes

Double tiger lily *(Lilium tigrinum flore pleno)* 'Honeysuckle Cottage' Grose Vale, NSW

Anthemis tinctoria

Paeonia suffruticosa × 'Comtesse de Tudor' (1856)

After clematis, what else? Not much for many gardeners (even in Colonial times there were plenty of one-eyed gardeners), but other climbers have their charms and their devotees. In tropical climes Bougainvilleas were *the* climbers and even in temperate areas they were widely planted. Just how many varieties were in commerce a hundred years ago is uncertain. Lists with a dozen or so sorts seem to have the usual purple, red, pink, white and variegated types. The teaser is in the small print underneath: 'Other varieties on application, plus newer novelties in short supply' and, 'Some other recent introductions' which tantalise and confound. Were there nineteenth century equivalents of our modern dwarf, double and parti-coloured forms? It seems highly likely to me that such cultivars were in existence, bearing in mind the passion, leisure and wealth with which some Colonial gardeners could pursue their hobby, and the extent and sophistication of the native nurseries of the Far East, near at hand and ready to satisfy the planters' whims and accept their patronage.

There yet remains a goodly selection of other climbers which produce a permanent framework, as well as perennial and annual climbers. Foremost among those which make a permanent growth are the jasmines, as popular today as they have ever been for their pervasive perfume, especially welcome on still summer evenings. Although there are real jasmines (*Jasminum* spp.), quite a few plants known as jasmines belong to other families; *Cestrum* spp. (Day and Night Jasmines), *Trachelospermum* (the Star Jasmine) and also the Confederate Jasmine, and the Carolina Yellow Jessamine, *Gelsemium*. The real jasmines known in the nineteenth century were *Jasminum sambac* and its double form, *J. gracilis, J. grandiflorum, J. officinale, J. poicoceum* and *J.* 'Maid of Orleans'—a double form I would like to meet. Other possiblities, if you still have some room left on a wall somewhere, are Stephanotis and Mandevilla.

Honeysuckles too were a family of climbers well known in those times. Some are very exuberant, so be careful to select varieties which will suit the space you have available. Two commonly found in old nursery catalogues are the very well known *Lonicera aureo-reticulata* and *L. confusa*, both evergreens and prodigious performers. The Early Dutch Honeysuckle *(L. periclymenum* v. *belgica)* and the Late Dutch Honeysuckle *(L. p. serotina)* are both well perfumed and have similar flowers, purple-red outside and creamy yellow within. The Trumpet Honeysuckle, *L. sempervirens* va. *superba* (also *magnifica*) has recently been introduced here and deserves inclusion. It has been known in English gardens since 1656 when it was introduced from the United States. It's odd that it isn't recorded here, as far as I can discern, for it certainly would have been well established in England by the nineteenth century. It has circular, paired leaves which are grey and often joined around the stem; the flowers are bright orange-red and tubular. There is no scent but it's still worthwhile.

In tropical and semi-tropical areas, the Passionflowers were well known, while in cooler frost-free areas they were frequently listed as climbers for sheltered corners and cool glasshouses. Among those listed in the late 1890s were these:

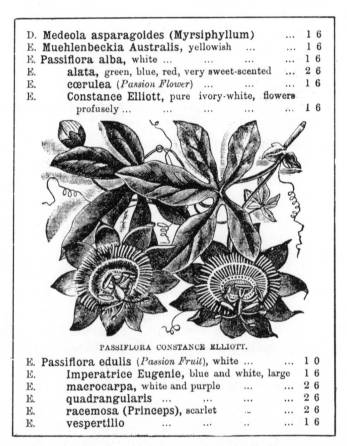

D.	Medeola asparagoides (Myrsiphyllum)	...	1 6
E.	Muehlenbeckia Australis, yellowish ...	...	1 6
E.	Passiflora alba, white	...	1 6
E.	alata, green, blue, red, very sweet-scented	...	2 6
E.	cœrulea (Passion Flower)	...	1 6
E.	Constance Elliott, pure ivory-white, flowers profusely	...	1 6

PASSIFLORA CONSTANCE ELLIOTT.

E.	Passiflora edulis (Passion Fruit), white ...	...	1 0
E.	Imperatrice Eugenie, blue and white, large		1 6
E.	macrocarpa, white and purple ...	...	2 6
E.	quadrangularis	...	2 6
E.	racemosa (Princeps), scarlet ..	...	2 6
E.	vespertilio	...	1 6

From a nineteenth-century catalogue

Colonial gardeners were also fond of tender climbers which could be treated as annuals. In some seasons these might come through the winter and make good re-growth; in others new seedlings would be needed to start the plants again. Two such that are still moderately popular are the Cup and Saucer Vine (Cobea scandens) and the Moonflower (Calonyction aculeatum), but what has happened to the curious green cobea from San Salvador that appeared in seed lists at the turn of the century? Its strange pendant flowers with very long stamens and thin twisted petals would make it a talking point

Cobea hookerana

in any modern cottage garden. It is probably either *Cobea hookerana* or *C. penduliflora*. *Eccremoncarpus scaber*, in yellow, orange and red strains, was another fairly reliable tender climber. They are still available (Thompson Morgan have them) but are not much seen.

One reliable perennial climber is Hops, but who sells it these days—to gardeners anyway? There are golden and variegated varieties but these seem quite lost as far as Australia goes. A pity, as both the foliage and fruits are attractive; it was grown for use in home brewing and home medicine.

The perennial peas have become naturalised in many parts of southern Australia, particularly the two-toned purple-red *Lathyrus tingitana*. The old-fashioned sweet peas, grown before a certain Mr Spencer started breeding them into today's large ruffled brands, may still be found in many old gardens. Their perennial roots live many years and they seed moderately too. These are *Lathyrus odoratus* and come in white, pale pink and rose and some intermediate forms with deeper coloured keels and lighter guard petals. The pure white form is particularly beautiful.

In favoured gardens where cool climate and acid soil are found, the Flame Creeper can be grown. It is a Tropaeolum and therefore a relative of the nasturtium. *T. tricolor* has small nodding red flowers with a single spur, and black and yellow markings at the mouth. The ferny leaves are trifoliate like miniature clover leaves. It grows from a dahlia-like tuber which demands damp, sandy, peaty soil in a cool place. In spring, fine wiry stems shoot up,

Ipomaea imperialis aurata

entwining whatever is handy, and flowers appear in mid-summer. It produces a very startling show from very light growth. Grown among dark slow conifers, such as *Pinus mugho, Taxus baccata fastigiata* or *Picea abies maxwellii*, it is especially brilliant.

Altogether more far-ranging are the Morning Glories (*Ipomaea* spp.). Our forebears knew white, red and Japanese forms as well as the familiar blues. The Japanese sorts are very large flowered in all sorts of colour variations including striped and flaked. Owing to our quarantine laws few other than the white and blue are available today. As they are such free and exceedingly strong growers they need care in placement, and even then should be kept out of small gardens.

As a last climber we could mention the gourds, those members of the cucumber and pumpkin family whose variegated fruits in curious shapes and covered with warts have been objects of fascination for ages. Though not so decorative as to warrant a prominent site in a garden, a few vines planted over a hen-house or by the back fence will provide an ample supply of decorative fruits for indoors. The vines are annuals and need good soil preparation and ample water during early summer.

The range of climbers grown in modern gardens seems much smaller than those grown in Colonial gardens. I would hazard a guess that a good many modern gardens have no climbers at all; I think it would be rare to find a nineteenth century garden that did not contain a grape-vine or even a lowly choko!

7 Gardens Curious...

We come finally to a sort of garden not often seen, though quite often enough according to some, and one which as a style relies not on plants for the material from which it is made but on objects. I refer to gardens made of collected bits and pieces such as you can see when you least expect to in seaside towns, country hamlets and suburban byways. These gardens are not so much grown as constructed and although the materials may have changed over the years seem no less popular than they were in the last century. The distinctive feature of these gardens are their diversity and the utilisation of everyday objects and 'found' things. Frequently the gardens comprise rockeries, grottoes, fishponds and rockwork constructed from pieces gathered by the folk of the household in the pursuit of their work and hobbies. Thus in mining areas extraordinary displays of various rock and mineral samples may be found displayed by being incorporated in cemented garden structures. In coastal towns flotsam and jetsam such as glass net floats, pieces of driftwood, whalebones, corals, shells and giant crab claws are utilised in garden decoration while in rural areas old farm wagons and ploughs or odds and ends welded into whimsical creations are employed. Everywhere, but particularly in the bigger towns and cities, the only too well known cement statue battalions take over a few gardens; brigades of rabbits shelter in forests of mushrooms while squads of flamingo stalk gnome armies amid a landscape of balustrades, urns, plinths, Japanese lanterns, assorted gods and goddesses, and dozing Mexicans.

As far as nineteenth century gardens are concerned the important thing to remember about gardens of whimsy is that they did exist and were generally constructed from collected bits and pieces rather than made from bought manmade objects. Thus objects covered with a glittering collection of glass, china and mirror pieces could be appropriate in a Victorian era garden but a collection of garden statuary would not; shell and crystal covered work would be suited to the spirit of the age but Italianate fountains, waterfalls and Japanese pieces generally would not do; pebble work, cobbling, rustic woodwork or even tin windmills and whirligigs may well find a place in an exceptional restored garden while decorations assembled from hubcaps and radiator grilles and bumper bars, however curious and inventive, would be completely wrong. If perchance you happen to have some bent towards making a garden of whimsicality then a careful selection of appropriate material will need to be gathered for use. Some objects such as a variety of rocks may be easily obtained but the likes of whalebones, lumps of crystal and old farm wagons will be decidedly most difficult and may also now be regarded as more valuable by antique and bric-a-brac collectors than by you. I rather think the cost of such a project might be daunting—perhaps just as well, going by the attitudes of many 'refined' gardeners and restorers who gladly enough erect Cape Cod weather vanes atop sheds but think precious little of own home-grown devices created with

Topiary scrollwork, Mt Bischoff, Tasmania, about 1900. Note the tin mines in the background. Courtesy Mrs Diana Morgan

our own motifs. The surprise created by gardens such as these, if gardens they be (are they not more often like outdoor extensions of the owner's magpie proclivities?), is a useful diversion from rural and urban sameness but it is their rarity that makes them noteworthy, far less than the objects they contain or the manner of their composition. Generally speaking the distribution of such displays is just about right to spice up our gardening lives; many more would be a freak show.

It is hard to say much more about such 'gardens' for they are really not easily discussed other than on an individual basis detailing structures, methods of construction, layout and the variety of materials used—all just a little too far removed from matters horticultural. There are, however, several other sorts of garden which are regarded as curious and related to our nineteenth century theme: they are cactus gardens and topiary gardens.

Cactus gardens seem to be almost unique to Australia, though I am certain that they may be found in isolated instances in other temperate climates such as South Africa, the Mediterranean and California, but whereas in the former and the latter they were extensions of a general interest in plants native to those zones, and in the Riviera the sportive tricks of very wealthy gardeners, in Australia they seem to have exerted a strange and compelling interest over small garden owners. Doubtless some of this influence was brought about by a generally harsh climate and a need for plants tough enough to survive it, perhaps too the migration of gold prospectors between the Cape, California and Australia played its part in familiarising home gardeners with these curious plants. While almost every garden had one or two aloes and possibly several clumps of columnar and barrel cacti, and almost certainly one or two clusters of Century Plant (*Agave americana*) a great deal of interest in these plants was also displayed in the horticultural papers of the day; and just as there were a few people interested in making gardens from the curiosities of the marine and minerological worlds there were a like-minded few interested in making gardens from the oddities of the plant world. So were gathered in aeoniums from the Canary Islands, aloes, crassula, Mesembryanthemum (Pig-face), Euphorbia and Stapelia from South Africa; Echeveria, Melocactus, Cereus, Mammillaria, Echinopsis, Cephalocereus, Hamatocactus, Echinocereus and half a hundred others from the Americas to adorn gardens with their gaunt, compelling forms and brilliant silken flowers—not to mention the much cursed Prickly Pear which rapidly took over large areas of hot dry pasture land when it was introduced as a fodder substitute in the last years of the nineteenth century. Planted up with all the formality of the biscuit-cutter beds—circles, stars and ovals outlined with rocks—these tough plants gave colour where ambitions must otherwise have been thwarted by lack of water. Within the beds rose columns taller than organ pipes; some naked, others fiercely spined and yet others covered in long hairs; great barrels of green laced over with a network of cast-iron fish-hooks and broad mats of close clustered fine-spined fat bodies creating marvels of symmetry—enough to satisfy the most enthusiastic whimsicologist!

Topiary, that art of cutting, pruning and training trees and shrubs to grow in predetermined shapes, has found few devotees if old records are anything to go by, for although we may find ample evidence for hedging and edging using trimmed plants there seems to have been little time for more frivolous works. As a child I can recall the fascination of several places where hedges of cypress were embellished with the name of the house cut from the greenery, over-arched at the gateway and beset with a pair of vaguely bird-shaped pieces, but these gardens would not have been made until the very early 1900s. There were also a table and two arm chairs cut from privet in one small garden and a migrant scandalised the neighbourhood by trimming ivy trained over his mail-box into a female torso (but that was in the 1950s, too late by far to be of much importance here). From photographic records the topiary that was made was usually of the simplest design and carried out in the houses where professional gardeners were employed. One may find examples of ivy trained up tree-ferns and palm trunks and cut into bottle and umbrella shapes, or in drier climes trained over wire baskets and umbrella forms and kept neatly cut.

Ivy seems to have been a very popular choice probably because effects of great age could be achieved in a very short time and because the traditional materials, box and yew, were not always easy to grow and usually not available in quantity or advanced sizes. In tropical areas bougainvillea seems to have been a popular substitute and allowing for its greater vigour probably suited very well.

From our photograph, taken at Mt Bischoff in Tasmania at the turn of the century, we can see that trimmed edging plants were a feature, and we may presume from similar photographs taken in other parts that such things were not uncommon. The choice of plants to carry out such schemes was catholic, encompassing dianthus, thymes and ivy as well as the more usual rosemary, lavender, santolina, *Rosa chinensis* and a dwarf strain of *Rosa multiflora* (Fairy Rose). Sometimes an alternative treatment was followed that would today seem odd; that was to build little banks of earth along the desired shapes and to puddle over a clay slurry which was smoothed and allowed to dry. As in an earlier chapter I described how edging plants were used in conjunction with others to plant up a garden bed I won't go over old ground again. In gardens where trimmed plants made up the whole creation the ground was usually 'decorated' with coloured gravels, pebbles, shell-grit, etc. I do not know if such 'knot gardens', as they were known, were decorated with crushed coloured glass and different colours of broken tile and brick as advocated by some English writers, but I am sure that like their modern day counterparts, who went in for pine-bark, river stones and the like, they found the constant picking off of leaves and papers a tiresome and unrewarding chore.

Most gardeners who regard themselves as sensitive to the beauties of foliage, flowers and form cannot take seriously those who make gardens out of curious objects and whimsical collections; however, they have had some small place in the development of cottage and villa gardens and so cannot be omitted. As they are the very unique creations of individuals with their own special perception of what their garden is about it is perhaps as well that few such gardens long survive their makers. The only well preserved genuine nineteenth century garden of curios that I know is to be found at The Olde Curiosity Shoppe in Ballarat. A visit there would be instructive in helping any prospective garden restorer to appreciate the attitude of gardeners of yesteryear to their task. Not all were highly refined in their selection of plants and materials, nor yet were all adept at throwing together a glorious display of mixed cottage plants—some were simply entranced by the intrinsic beauty of curious objects and fascinated by the potential of everyday flotsam and jetsam for creating items of whimsy.

POSTSCRIPT

For me, the work is largely done; for you, I hope this will be a starting point in your own restoration project for the garden of your Colonial home. No doubt you will find some things I've left out, but then this wasn't mean to be an encyclopaedic work, and finding out for yourself is an important part of the enjoyment waiting for you.

Good luck!

APPENDIX 1

Trees, Shrubs and Herbs Common in the Nineteenth Century

The common plants grown in gardens with a Mediterranean climate in the nineteenth century divided into herbs, shrubs and trees, and including a number of non-European exotics.

HERBS

Allium moly
Amaryllis belladonna (S. Africa)
Anemone appeinina, coronaria
Antirrhinum majus
Aster spp.
Campanula pyramidalis, rapunculoides, trachelium
Canna indica
Colchicum autumnale
Consolida regalis
Crocus spp.
Cyclamen neapolitanum, persicum
Celosia cristata
Centaurea cyanus, moschata
Dictamnus albus
Digitalis purpurea, grandiflora, lutea
Eranthis hyemalis
Erythronium dens-canis
Fragaria vesca, virginiana (N. America)
Fritillaria imperialis, meleagris
Galanthus nivalis
Helianthus tuberosus, annus (N. America)
Heliotropium peruvianum
Helleborus niger
Iris xiphium

Impatiens balsamina
Leonotus leonurus
Leucojum aestivum
Lilium chalcedonicum, martagon, candidum
Lychnis coeli-rosa
Mirabilis jalapa (S. America)
Matthiola spp.
Muscari botryoides
Monarda didyma
Nicotiana tabacum (S. America)
Narcissus spp.
Ornithogalum umbellatum
Paeonia albiflora
Pelargonium spp.
Philadelphus coronarius
Polemonium caeruleum
Rosa centifolia, eglanteria, damascena, canina
Ranunculus asiaticus
Scabiosa atropurpurea
Scilla peruviana
Tulipa spp. cv.
Tagetes erecta (Mexico)
Tropaeolum majus
Xeranthemum spp.

SHRUBS

Campsis radicans (N. America)
Citrus spp.
Convolvulus spp.
Cytisus albus
Hibiscus mutabilis, rosa-sinensis (tropics)
Jasminum odoratissimum, sambac

Passiflora edulis
Prunus cerasus, persica
Syringa vulgaris
Viburnum opulus cv. 'Sterile'
Yucca gloriosa (N. America)

Herbs and woody plants basic to Mediterranean gardening are:

HERBS

Acanthus mollis
Aconitum napellus
Althaea rosea
Anthemis nobilis
Asphodeline lutea
Artemisia abrotanum
Borago officinalis
Calendula officinalis
Celosia cristata
Centaurea cyanus
Chrysanthemum coronarium, segetum,
　grandiflorum
Cistus ladanifer
Crocus sativus
Convallaria majalis
Dianthus plumarius, caryophyllus
Digitalis purpurea
Foeniculum officinale
Gladiolus segetum
Hyssopus officinalis
Hesperis matronalis
Hyacinthus orientalis

Iris florentina, germanica, pseudacorus
Jasminum officinale
Lavandula offincalis
Lilium candidum, martagon
Lychnis coronaria
Melissa officinalis
Nigella damascena
Narcissus poeticus
Origanum marjorana
Paeonia officinalis
Papaver rhoeas, somniferum
Portulaca oleraea
Primula auricula, vulgaris
Rosa alba, centifolia, damascena, gallica
Ruta graveolens
Senecio cineraria
Symphytum officinale
Teucrium fruticans
Thymus serpyllum, vulgaris
Vinca minor
Viola odorata, tricolor

SHRUBS

Crataegus monogyna
Cytisus scoparius
Danaea racemosus
Lonicera periclymenum

Rosmarinus officinale
Ruscus aculeatus
Sambucus nigra
Viburnum tinus

TREES

Arbutus unedo
Buxus sempervirens
Cornus mas
Cupressus sempervirens
Cydonia oblonga
Hedera helix
Laurus nobilis
Myrtus communis

Nerium oleander
Phoenix dactylifera
Platanus orientalis
Punica granatum
Prunus amygdalus, cerasus, persica
Pyrus communis
Malus baccata
Pistacia lentiscus

GARDEN TREES

Magnolia; Illicium; Berberis; Pittosporum; Camellia; Aesculus; Ilex; Rhamnus; Crataegus; Photinia; Rosa; Hedera; Viburnum; Aucuba; Arbutus; Rhododendron; Laurus; Buxus; Quercus; Fagus; Olea; Phillyrea; Syringa; Fraxinus; Texus; Pinus; Abies; Picea; Thuja; Taxodium; Juniperus.

OTHERS IN POTS
Fuchsia; Myrtus; Dahlia; Pelargonium.

PADDOCK TREES

Acer pseudoplatanus, negundo   *Mespilus germanica*
Aesculus carnea   *Populus balsamifera*
Alnus glutinosa   *Quercus cerris, ilex*
Amelanchier canadensis   *Robinia pseudoacacia*
Betula alba   *Salix alba*
Crataegus crus-gallii   *Sorbus aria, aucuparia*
Fraxinus ornus   *Taxodium distichum*
Gleditschia triacanthos   *Tilia × europaea*
Laburnum alpinum

By permission of Dr Brian Morley, Director, Adelaide Botanic Gardens from his lecture to the First Garden History
Conference, Melbourne, 1980.

APPENDIX 2

Camellias

This short list represents Australian raised hybrids of Colonial days. The plants
were mainly raised in the Sydney region by Sir William Macarthur, Michael
Guilfoyle, T.W. Shepherd and Silas Sheather. These same growers imported many
other contemporary cultivars from Italy, Belgium, Japan, France, Germany and the
United States of America. (For full details see Stirling Macoboy, *The Colour
Dictionary of Camellias*, Lansdowne, Sydney 1981.)

'Aspasia' – 1850, double creamy-white, some streaking.
'Cassandra' — 1850, scarlet-crimson.
'Cleopatra' — 1850, white striped pink.
'Dido' – 1861, white semi-double.
'Great Eastern' – 1873, hose-in-hose rose-red.
'Harriet Beecher Sheather' – 1872, formal rose-salmon.
'Hellenor' – 1866, pale pink, flecked and striped.
'Lady Loch' – 1898, informal pale pink, white edges.
'Leviathan' – 1862, deepset rose-red, paeony form.
'Prince Frederick William' – 1872, formal rose-pink.
'Speciosissima' – 1862, pure carmine-red.
'Tabbs' – 1856, crimson marbled white.
'Virginia Franco Rosea' – 1875, formal rich rose, paler edges.
'Zambo' – 1874, formal mauve-pink.

APPENDIX 3

Favourite Nineteenth Century Roses

Once-flowering Roses—Usually in Early Summer

'Chapeau de Napoleon' – 1827, unusual Moss rose, warm pink.

'Charles de Mills' – 1800, low shrubby plant, fully double beetroot-purple flowers.

'Fortune's Double Yellow' – 1845, modest climber, apricot-yellow flowers with rosy veins, *Rosa* × *odorata pseudindica*.

'James Mitchell' – 1861, lilac-pink Moss rose.

'James Veitch' – 1865, violet-slate shaded maroon, large-flowers Moss rose.

'Old Pink Moss' – 1727, *Rosa centifolia muscosa*, warm pink flowers.

'Rosa Mundi' – pre-1500, low bush, flowers light pink striped bright pink fading to lilac (Gallica).

'Tuscany' – pre-1600, low bush, flowers dark crimson with gold stamens showing (Gallica).

Repeat-flowering Roses

'Boule de Neige' – 1867, pure white pompom-shaped flowers (Bourbon).

'Caroline de Sansal' – 1849, pink with a darker rose-pink centre (Hybrid Perpetual).

'Comtesse du Cayla' – 1902, vibrant rose, apricot, flame and nasturtium-red, semi-double (China).

'Cramoisi Superieur' – 1832, bright red-crimson, semi-double, also known as 'Aggripina' (China).

'Crepuscule' – 1904, semi-double apricot yellow, modest climber (Noisette).

'Duchesse de Brabant' – 1857, semi-double pearly-pink (China).

'La Reine' – 1842, large double-cupped pink (Bourbon).

'Louis XIV' – 1859, dark crimson, double, low bush (China).

'Mme Ernst Calvat' – 1888, pale pink, deeper rose centre (Bourbon)

'Mme Isaac Pereire' – 1881, deep madder rose, large and double (Bourbon).

'Mrs John Laing' – the 'Cabbage Rose' of colonial days. Large double pink (Hybrid Perpetual).

'Old Blush' – 1759, semi-double two-tone pink, always in bloom, also known as 'Common Monthly', 'Old Pink Daily', 'Old Pink Monthly', 'Parson's Pink China' (China).

'Paul Neyron' – 1869, rich pink, large and double (Hybrid Perpetual).

'Perle d'Or' – 1883, apricot button-hole rose, similar to 'Cecile Brunner' (China).

'Princesse de Sagan' – 1887, velvety crimson shaded purplish (China).

'Reine Victoria' – 1872, the 'Shell Rose', cupped warm pink passing to lilac-pink, also known as 'La Reine Victoria' (Bourbon).

Tea Roses—The Nonpareils of Nineteenth Century Roses

'Adam' – 1833, apricot-pink, similar to 'Devoniensis' but better growth, climber.

'Archduke Charles' – 1840, rosy crimson marbled pink.

'Archiduc Joseph' – 1872, purplish-pink with paler pink heart.

'Baronne Henriette de Snoy' – 1897, flesh pink with darker reverse, strong grower.

'Devoniensis' – 1838, creamy blush apricot, the 'Magnolia Rose', also a climbing form.

'Dr Grill' – 1886, rose pink with some coppery tones.

'Francis Dubreuil' – 1894, velvety crimson.

'General Gallieni' – 1899, maroon with brighter coppery tones.

'Grace Darling' – 1884, cream shaded pink, strong grower.

'Isabella Sprunt' – 1865, semi-double creamy-yellow, sport of 'Safrano'.

'Laurette Messimy' – 1887, rose-pink shaded yellow, also known as 'Mme Laurette Messimy'.

'Marie van Houtte' – 1871, deep cream tinged pink at edges.

'Mme Charles' – 1864, multi-flowered pink with yellow centre, semi-double.

'Molly Sharman Crawford' – 1908, full-petalled white, creamy-flesh centre, sometimes greenish (possibly known in Australia as 'Monty's White').

'Monsieur Tillier' – 1891, fully double coppery pink.

'Mrs B.R. Cant' – 1901, fully double rose pink.

'Mrs Dudley Cross' – 1907, pale chamois-cream shaded crimson in cool weather.

'Mrs Foley Hobbs' – 1910, ivory-white tinted pink at the edges.

'Niphetos' – 1843, pure white climber.

'Noella Nabonnand' – 1901, silky vivid deep pink, vigorous.

'Safrano' – 1839, saffron and apricot yellow.

'Sombreuil' – 1850, pure white, fully double, climber.

'Souvenir d'un Ami' – 1846, rose pink tinted salmon.

APPENDIX 4

Paeonies

Herbaceous Paeonies

'Duchesse de Nemours' – 1856, double white.
'Festiva Maxima' – 1851, double white, flecked red.
'Marie Crousse' – 1892, pale pink double.
'Monsieur Jules Elie' – 1888, deep pink double.
'Felix Crousse' – 1881, double red.
'Sarah Bernhardt' – 1906, rich pink double.

Tree Paeonies

Tree paeonies were available at 4/6 each in the 1880s but it is not clear from catalogues I have seen whether these were named Japanese or European varieties or if they were seedlings. Even today plants are hard to get and frequently choice is limited to one or two varieties only, so you must take what you can get—a list of preferred varieties would be almost impossible to fulfill and most likely cause embarrassment. If you are at all green-fingered tree paeonies are quite easily raised from seed but will take about five years to bloom.

APPENDIX 5

Favourite Shrubs

Lilacs (Syringa)
Syringa velutina – dwarf bush, pinky mauve flowers (1910).
S. *persica* – small white flowers (1640)
S. × 'Belle de Nancy' – large double lavender.
S. × 'Charles Joly' – double reddish-purple (1896)
S. × 'Jan Van Tol' – large single white.
S. × 'Mme Lemoine' – double white (1890)
S. × 'President Grevy' – double blue.
S. × 'Souvenir de Louis Spaeth' – single purple (1883)

The following lists are taken from late nineteenth century catalogues.

Philadelphus
Philadelphus coronarius (Mock Orange), white
P. grandiflorus, white
P. g. speciocissimus plenus, large double white flowers, deliciously scented
P. inodorus, large white, very pretty
P. mexicanus, white
P. multiflorus plenus, double white
P. speciosa, white
   Handsome sweet-scented shrubs, flowering in spring; well adapted for bouquets.

Spiraea
Spiraea 'Anthony Waterer', bright rose
S. bumaldi, rose
S. corymbolosa (May), white
S. douglasi, rose
S. grandiflora (exochorda), large white
S. lindleyana, white
S. nobleana, rose
S. prunifolia, double white
S. reevesiana, double white
S. thunbergi, white
   Very hardy shrubs, blooming freely early in Spring.

Oleander
Nerium (Oleander) 'Delphine', deep rich crimson
N. album plenum, semi-double white
N. album grandiflorum, white
N. carneum, red
N. grandiflorum plenum, very large double, pink
N. 'Madame Martin', beautiful clear salmon (Hose in Hose)
N. madoni grandiflorum, large pure white, semi-double
N. 'Professor Martin', crimson, dwarf, and compact; single crimson; white
N. 'Souvenir de Cazalis Allut', extremely rich crimson, the darkest of all
N. splendens, double pink
N. splendens variegata, handsome variegated leaves
   Very hardy ornamental shrubs, flowering profusely during the Summer.

Bouvardias

'Alfred Neuner', double, pure white, like a miniature Tuberose, large compact trusses. Excellent for bouquets.

Angustifolia, brilliant scarlet, medium-size flower, free-flowering. Well adapted for buttonholes, &c.

'Beauty of Brisbane'. A pure snow white sport from *Priory Beauty*. 2s. 6d.

'Beauty of New South Wales', a hybrid between *Humboldti corymbiflora* and *Priory Beauty*; creamy white, base of petals and calyx flesh colour, large broad petals, massive flower. 2s. 6d.

'Bridal Wreath', large clusters snow-white flowers.

Candidissima, pure white, sweetly scented

Conspicua, bright blood-red, whitish tube; the pistil extending beyond the flowers like a white star.

'Dazzler', large, rich scarlet flowers, free.

Elegans, intense vermilion scarlet, very rich and bright

'Etna', large double reddish vermilion.

Flavescens, pale yellow, the finest of its colour, free and distinct

Flavescens flore pleno, fine large double yellow, vigorous.

'Hogarth', large clusters of scarlet flowers, good habit.

'Hogarth' *flore pleno*, a beautiful double-flowered form of the useful and well-known B. *Hogarth*. The flowers are bright red, very double, and prettily imbricated.

Humboldti corymbiflora, pure white flowers, delightfully scented, like Orange-blossoms. One of the finest.

Humboldti corymbiflora magnifica, snow white, extra fine.

'Laura', fine, rose-scented.

Leinantha splendens, crimson, very hardy.

'Maiden's Blush', bright blush pink, neat habit, profuse bloomer.

'Oriflamme', rich vermilion scarlet, very beautiful.

'President Cleveland', a splendid rich-coloured variety, fine large crimson-scarlet flowers, very bright colour.

'President Garfield', large trusses of double pink flowers, good habit, and profuse bloomer.

'Priory Beauty', a beautiful shade of pale satin rose, flowers freely produced in large trusses.

'Triomphe de Nancy', vigorous and free-flowering, with large, compact trusses of well-formed, double, beautiful, orange-salmon flowers.

Umbellata Carnea, creamy white, changing to rosy blush; very fragrant.

'Unique', rosy pink, white throat, broad petals slightly recurved, long white tube.

'Van Houttei', rich red; very free.

'Victor Lemoine', the fine imbricated double flowers of this variety are of a fiery scarlet; produced in large corymbs.

Vreelandi (syn. *Davisoni*), pure white, sweet-scented. Invaluable for bouquets.

And some other varieties.

Lantana

Lantana alba, white
L. crocea, red
L. 'Sellowi', purple
L. 'Le Nain', red, orange centre
L. 'Goliath', orange and red
L. 'Imperatrice Eugenie', rose and cream
L. 'Ne plus ultra', red, orange centre
L. 'Pretension', creamy white, centre brilliant yellow
L. 'Princess Louise', crimson, orange centre
L. 'Rougiere Chauviere', orange and red; very fine
L. sanguinea, red and orange
L. sulphurea, yellow, changing to rich carmine
L. 'Triomphe de l'Exposition', white
L. 'Triomphe du Commerce', bronze yellow, bright red centre, changing to lilac violet
L. 'Vulcan', rose colour, light centre
   And others. All very free-flowering shrubs.

Begonias

Evergreen (Flowering Varieties)
Argyrostigma, white, pale-green foliage
Corallina, coral red
Credneri, pink
Dregii, white
Froebeli, large brilliant scarlet
Florida incomparabilis, white dwarf
'Gloire de Sceaux', rose, metallic foliage, splendid Winter flowering variety
Hybrida floribunda, rosy pink, very pretty
Hydrocotylifolia, pink
Lucida, white
Metallica
Meyeri, white
Nitida, pink
Picta, white
Platanifolia, white
Ricinifolia maculata, red
Schmidti, white
Semperflorens alba, white
Semperflorens rosa, pale rose
Sulcata, white
Sutherlandi, orange
Undulata, white
Weltoniensis, pink
Zebrina

PALMS AND CYCADS.

N.B.—The Prices of all Palms vary according to size and age.

WE HAVE A GRAND STOCK OF PALMS OF VARIOUS SIZES, AND INVITE INSPECTION.

ARECA BAUERI.

CHAMÆROPS EXCELSA.

Price.

Areca Baueri, very hardy, large handsome leaves 2/- to   3 6
     lustescens   ...   ...   5/- to   7 6
     monostachya 3 6
     sapida ("*The Nikau Palm*"), one of the finest of N.Z. trees, and very decorative, 6 to 10 ft.   3 6
Brahea edulis, a new Fan-Palm from *Guadaloupe*   7 6
     glauca (*Blue Palm*), very ornamental Fan-Palm, bright green leaves, glaucous beneath; new and rare 7 6
Caryota sobolifera   ...   ...   2/6 to   5 0
     urens (*Wine Palm*)   ...   2/6 to   5 0
Chamærops Excelsa, one of the hardiest of the Fan-Palms, dark green foliage, the segments of the fan-shaped leaves deeply cut, the edges covered with tooth-like spines, very desirable for out-door decoration ...   2/6 to   5 0
     Chamærops Fortunei 3 6
     humilis, large grand, fan-shaped leaves, of dwarf habit, a splendid specimen for the lawn   ...   2/6 to   5 0
Cocos plumosa   ...   ...   2/6 to   7 6
     Weddelliana, the most elegant of all the smaller Palms; very graceful table plant   ...   5/- to   10 6
Corypha Australis, graceful Fan Palm, very useful and hardy, also known as "Cabbage-Tree Palm." Foliage dark green, very symmetrically and regularly slit; the segments partly doubled from base of petioles or leaf stalk, which is thickly armed with crooked spines ...   2/6 to   5 0
Cycas revoluta, very elegant   ...   ...   5/- to   10 6
Kentia Belmoreana (*Howea Belmoreana*), this fine Palm has dark green Pinnate leaves, very elegant and graceful, a native of Lord Howe's Island   ...   2/6 to   5 0
Kentia Canterburyana (*Hedyscepe Canterburyana*)   3/6 to   5 0
Kentia Forsteriana (*Howea Forsteriana*), elegant   2/6 to   5 0
Latania Borbonica, large fan-shaped leaves, much divided, very handsome ...   .   3/6 to   20 0
Macrozamia spiralis "Barrawang"   ...   3/6 to   7 6
Phœnix canariensis, very handsome, rapid grower, dark green pinnate leaves, lance shaped, much pointed; hardy   3/6 to   5 0
     humilis   ...   .   3/6 to   7 6
     dactylifera (*Date Palm*)   ...   ...   2/6 to   7 6

CORYPHA AUSTRALIS.

KENTIA BELMOREANA.

KENTIA FORSTERIANA.

PHŒNIX RECLINATA.

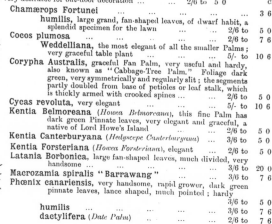

WASHINGTONIA ROBUSTA (PRITCHARDIA).

Phœnix reclinata, very graceful. A very fine large-growing species; leaves pinnate; largely used in the south of France for avenues; hardy   2/6 to   7 6
     rupicola   ...   2/6 to   20 0
     sylvestris   ...   3/6 to   5 0
Pritchardia filifera (*Brahea filamentosa*), very handsome; hardy ...   2/6 to   7 6
Pritchardia grandis (*Licuala*)
Ptychosperma Alexandræ, quick grower, very handsome 3 6

Z

Rhapis flabelliformis, a delicate and graceful little Palm; from China and Japan 7 6
Sabal Adansoni   2/6 to   5 0
     Blackburniana (*umbraculifera*) 3 6
Seaforthia elegans, long, arching, graceful, dark green leaves, a most elegant species   ...   2/6 to   7 6
Washingtonia filifera   2/6 to   7 6
     robusta   ...   3/6 to   7 6

APPENDIX 7

ORANGE, LEMON AND OTHER CITRUS TREES.

1s. 6d. to 2s. each, according to size of trees.   Larger size trees can be supplied.

Special quotations for large quantities.

Acme, fruit large, round, solid, fine flavour

Blood, or **Maltese**, medium size, pulp stained with deep crimson, thin skin, sweet, delicious flavour. One of the best

Cluster, fine. The fruit is produced in clusters

Maltese Oval, medium size, oval, fine flavour

Navel (*Bahia*), a great favourite ; fine large fruit of exquisite flavour ; seedless, but rather shy bearer

Oval China, large oval, light colour, skin thin, fine flavour

Parramatta, a well-known sort ; very large and prolific

Queen, large and good ; fine for market

Rio, large, solid, fine flavour

Sabina, large, dark skinned, fine flavoured, prolific

Siletta, medium size, good, very prolific

St. Jago, large and good

St. Michael, large, thin skinned, fine flavour. A great favourite

Teneriffe, medium size, roundish, fine quality

Washington Navel, said to be a great acquisition. 2s. 6d.

Allsop's Gem, medium size, excellent quality, skin smooth and thin, 2s.

Flower of Sydney, large, round, good quality. 2s.

Naranja Prata, thin skin, solid, excellent flavour, heavy cropper. 2s.

Mexicana, large, good flavour. 2s.

Mediterranean Sweet, a very popular variety in America. 2s.

Pernambucana, good size, heavy, fine quality. 2s.

MANDARIN ORANGES.   1s. 6d. to 2s.

Canton, large and prolific, fine flavour

Emperor, large, fine flavour

Emperor of China, fine, large

Japanese Seedless, large, early

Nobilis, medium size, flat, solid, good

Scarlet, large, very flat, fine colour

Thorny, small, solid, fine flavour

Willow-leaved

PRESERVING ORANGES.

Cumquat, small, round, very thin skinned, pleasantly bitter ; used for preserving. 2s. 6d.

Myrtle-leaved Orange, small, makes a very handsome Shrub. 2s.

Poor Man, fine large fruit, used for marmalade and candied peel. 1s. 6d.

Seville (*Citrus vulgaris*), bitter, largely used for marmalade, also for candied peel. 1s. 6d.

Tangierine, medium size, somewhat flattened, with very pleasant perfume and agreeably flavoured flesh. 2s. 6d.

ORANGES, &c.

BENGAL CITRON (*Citrus medica*), fine, large ; used for candied peel. 2s. to 2s. 6d.

KNIGHT'S CITRON, fruit long, rough skin, prolific. 2s.

LISBON LEMON (*Citrus limonum*), fine, large, thin-skinned, excellent flavour. This is the best of all Lemons, and the fruit is in great demand in the Summer

CHATSWORTH LISBON LEMON, said to be an improvement on the *Lisbon*. 2s.

VARIEGATED LISBON LEMON. The leaves and fruit are beautifully variegated, very ornamental ; fruit equal to the plain-leaved Lisbon Lemon

WEST INDIAN LIME (*Citrus limetta*), small and excellent, very thin skinned ; best for lime juice. 2s.

POMELOW. 2s.

SHADDOCK (*Citrus decumana*), very large ; used for candied peel. 2s.

Reproduced from a nineteenth century catalogue.

Pelargoniums

Flowering Zonal Pelargoniums (Geraniums)
'Prince of Wales' 1871, single, purple/magenta
'Jewel' 1875, double, scarlet/purple
'Mrs G. Ashworth' 1915, double, white
'Rev. F. Atkinson' 1890, single, deep crimson, nosegay type
'F.V. Raspail' 1885, double, deep scarlet
'King of Denmark' 1915, double, salmon pink
'Winston Churchill' 1915, single, magenta pink, large white eye
'Fraicheur' 1915, double, white flushed and margined pink
'Jean Viaud' 1916, double, soft pink
'Double Jacoby' 1889, double, deepest crimson
'Henry Jacoby' 1899, single, deepest crimson
'Madame Charlotte' 1899, semi-double, mottled salmon
'Nydia' 1899, double, white tinted cream, pink centre
'New Life' 1890, single, red and white

Ivy-Leaved Pelargoniums
'Beauty of Jersey' 1899, semi-double, vermilion
'Joseph Warren' 1899, double, rosy purple
'Souv. de Charles Turner' 1889, double, rosy cerise
'Beauty of Castlehill' 1899, double, soft rose
'Jeanne D'Arc' 1891, single, white, feathered
'Abel Carriere' 1898, semi-double, cerise
'Madame Crousse' 1891, double, silvery pink
'L'Elegante' 1871, single, white, feathered. Foliage white edged.
'Galilee' 1897, double, toothpaste pink
'Fürstin J. von Hohensollern' 1892, double, deep scarlet-red/magenta

Regal Pelargoniums
'Her Majesty' 1895, white
'Emperor of Russia' 1895, dark maroon crimson, white edge
'Madame Thibaut' 1885, ruffled white, blotched and speckled rose pink
'Gold Mine' 1897, orange scarlet, upper petals blotched
'Azalea' ('Azaleaflora') 1873, pink, colour of Splendens azalea.

Scented-Leaved Pelargoniums
P. tomentosum 1857, peppermint
P. crispum 1899, citron
P. fragrans 1897, nutmeg/spice
'Lady Plymouth' 1885, rose
P. capitatum 1885, supposedly rose
P. denticulatum 1885, pungent
P. graveolens 1892, rose
P. quercifolium 1892, pungent
'White Unique' 1892, not necessarily perfumed
'Rollison's Unique' 1885, not necessarily perfumed

Species Pelargoniums
(other than those listed above which are also classified as scented-leaved)
P. cucullatum flore pleno 1885, double purple
P. blandfordianum 1892, white or pink
P. carnosum 1892
P. echinatum stapletonii 1892
P. gibbosum 1892
P. triste 1892
P. vitifolium 1892

APPENDIX 9
Some Sources of Old-Fashioned Plants
(Trees, shrubs, climbers, bulbs, tubers, corms, roots, perennials and seeds.)

Trees, etc.

Chandlers Nursery
P.O. Box 13
The Basin, Vic. 3154

Newman's Nursery
North East Road
Tea Tree Gully, SA 5091

Arnold Teese
Yamina Rare Plants
25 Moores Road
Monbulk, Vic. 3793

*Camellia Lodge
348-350 Princes Hwy
Noble Park, Vic. 3174

Camellia Magic
1395 Old Northern Road
Dural, NSW 2158

Gillanders' Woodbank Nursery
RMB 303
Kingston, Tas. 7150

David Thompson (Rare trees,
Climbers and Perennials)
Gores Road
Summertown, SA 5154

Rumsey's Roses (Tea roses)
PO Box 1
Dural, NSW 2158

Ross Roses (Old roses)
P.O. Box 23
Willunga, SA 5172

The Flower Garden (Old roses)
P.O. Box 18
Watervale, SA 5452

Lesley Butler (Fuchsias)
21 Alphington Street
Alphington, Vic. 3078

*Charlie Szabo
The Green Witch Nursery
Avenue Road
Stirling, SA 5152

Dandenong Nurseries *(Geraniums)*
20 Maurice Street
Dandenong, Vic. 3175

Norton Summit Nurseries
Main Road
Norton Summit, SA 5136

*J.E. & E.P. Acot *(Standard box trees
and paeonies)*
Bowen Street
Trentham, Vic. 3458

The Lavender Patch
Cullens Road
Kincumber, NSW 2250

Erdman's Cottage
Lot 3, Church Street
Bundanoon, NSW 2578

*The Geranium House
Market Place
Berrima, NSW 2577

*Mrs Susan St Leon *(Own-root roses)*
'Bleak House'
Calder Highway
Malmsbury, Vic. 3446

*Garden of St Erth
Simmon's Reef
via Blackwood, Vic. 3458

Mrs June Morley *(Own-root roses)*
P.O. Box 138
Gumeracha, SA 5233

*N.B. These nurseries are not yet
able to provide a mail order service.

Perennials, Bulbs, etc.

Norgates Plant Farm
Blackwood Road
Trentham, Vic. 3458

J.N. Hancock & Co. *(Daffodils)*
Jackson Hill Road
Menzies Creek, Vic. 3159

Ken Bilston
83 Yarrowee Street
Sebastopol, Vic. 3356

Hahndorf County Garden
30 Main Street
Hahndorf, SA 5245

The Perennial Cottage Garden
Hume Highway
Berrima, NSW 2577

The Rose Arbour *(Cottage plants)*
154 Wattletree Road
Malvern, Vic. 3144

The Country Fields
167 Main Road
Belair, SA 5052

*Badger's Keep Nursery
(by appointment only)
Chewton, Vic. 3451
(ph. 054-72 3338)

Dr Judyth McLeod
'Honeysuckle Cottage'
Lot 35 Bowen Mountain Road
Bowen Mountain, NSW 2753

Meadows Herbs
Sims Road
Mount Barker, SA 5251

Woodside Herbs
R.M.B.100C
Georges River Road
Kentlyn, NSW 2560

The Fragrant Garden
Portsmouth Road
Erina, NSW 2250

Daylily Display Centre
203 Watson Road
Acacia Ridge, QLD. 4110

Coffield's Nursery *(Rock plants)*
c/o P.O.
Creswick, Vic. 3363

Neville J. Harrop *(Paeonies)*
17 Auvergne Avenue
Newtown, Tas. 7008

Tempo Two *(Day lilies and iris)*
Leongatha Road
Ellingbank, via Warragul, Vic.
3820

Warrimoo Iris Gardens
115 Craigend Street
Leura, NSW 2718

Rainbow Ridge Nursery *(Day lilies and iris)*
8 Taylors Road
Dural, NSW 2158

Borrika Bulbs *(South African and South American bulbs)*
P.O. Box 118
Murray Bridge, SA 5253

*Willunga Herbs—Nursery & Gardens
Bong Bong Hill
Moss Vale, NSW 2577

Delta County Iris Nursery
P.O. Box 121
Alstonville, NSW 2477

Deep Creek Herb Nursery
3 Deep Creek Road
Mitcham, Vic. 3132

*Bundanoon Village Nursery
71 Penrose Rd,
Bundanoon, NSW 2578

Seeds

Thompson & Morgan
c/- Erica Vale Australia P/L
P.O. Box 50
Jannali, NSW 2226

Digger Garden Club
105 Latrobe Parade
Dromana, Vic. 3936

M. McDougall *(Gawler sweet peas)*
Paris Creek
P.O. Box 63
Meadows, SA 5201

Chiltern Seeds, Dept. R
Boretree Stile
Ulverston
Cumbria LA12 7PB U.K.

Albion Botanicals Ltd *($4 for large catalogue)*
High St
Coton
Cambridge, U.K.

Dept. S6 *(Dianthus seed)*
Allwood Bros (Hassocks) Ltd
Hassocks
West Sussex, U.K.

Feathers Nursery *(South African plants and bulb seeds)*
P.O. Box 13
Constantia 7848
Republic of South Africa

Societies

Hardy Plant Society
c/- Miss B. White
10 St Barnabas Road
Emmer Green, Caversham,
Reading
United Kingdom

Heritage Roses in Australia
c/- Mr T. Nottle
5 Walker Street
Stirling, SA 5152

The Australian Garden History
Society
P.O. Box 588
Bowral, NSW 2576

Many of these businesses are small, personal nurseries and from time to time they change hands or cease trading. Once you have become thoroughly immersed in garden restoration, you will be aware of these changes and the many new businesses which spring up yearly. I have listed those places I have dealt happily with for many years. I am sure you will be able to add many more from the Blue Mountains, the Dandenongs, Mt Macedon and elsewhere. When writing to, or visiting these places, it is important to have a short list of things you want and to ask for them. It is equally important to keep your eyes open for other plants which may add to the treasure trove of your nineteenth century garden.

APPENDIX 10

Useful Reading

One of the many pleasures involved in restoring a garden, and in being a garden historian, is that you can hardly help getting into reading about gardening. For your pleasure, I list a few books which may help in your own garden restoration.

Journals

Australian Garden History Society, ed. Miranda Morris-Nunn, 1980–1983. (Now superseded by *The Australian Garden Journal*, ed. Tim North.)

Ebury, Lady (ed.), *Proceedings of the First Garden History Conference*, National Trust/AGHS, Melbourne, 1980.

Robinson, William, *Gardening Illustrated*, London, 1880.

Robinson, William, *Flora & Sylva* (three volumes), London, 1903–1905.

Books

Bligh, Beatrice: *Cherish the Earth*, Ure Smith, Sydney, 1975.

Cuffley, Peter: *Cottage Gardens in Australia*, 5-Mile Press, Melbourne, 1983.

Fish, Margery: *Cottage Garden Flowers*, Faber, London, 1981.

Genders, Roy: *The Cottage Garden and Old-Fashioned Flowers*, Pelham, London, 1983.

Gorer, Richard: *The Flower Garden in England*, Batsford/RHS, London, 1975.

Nottle, Trevor: *Growing Old-Fashioned Roses*, Kangaroo Press, Sydney, 1983.

Polya, Rosemary: *19th Centry Plant Nursery Catalogues of S.E. Australia*, La Trobe University, Melbourne, 1981.

McPhee Gribble: *An Australian Gardener's Anthology*, Rigby, Adelaide, 1982.

Robinson, William: *The English Flower Garden* (8th edition), John Murray, London, 1903.

Scott-James, Anne: *The Cottage Garden*, Allen Lane, London, 1981.

Tanner, Howard: *Converting the Wilderness – the art of gardening in colonial Australia* (catalogue), Australian Gallery Directors' Council, Sydney, 1979.

Thomas, Graham Stuart: *The Old Shrub Roses*, Phoenix House, London, 1959.

Thomas, Graham Stuart: *Climbing Roses Old and New*, Phoenix House, London, 1967.

BIBLIOGRAPHY

(Excluding the publications already listed)

Books and Journals

Beales, Peter: *Georgian and Regency Roses; Early Victorian Roses; Late Victorian Roses; Edwardian Roses*, Jarrold, Norwich, 1979.

Beames, R., & Whitehall, A.: *Some Historic Gardens of South Australia*, Adelaide Botanical Gardens/National Trust, Adelaide, 1981.

Britten, James: *European Ferns*, Cassel, London, 1875.

Burns, T., & Skenp, J.R. (eds.): *Van Diemen's Land Correspondents, 1827-1849*, Queen Victoria Museum, Launceston, 1961.

Coombs, Roy E.: *Violets*, Croom Helm, London, 1981.

Crittenden, Victor H.: *The Front Garden*, Mulini Press, Canberra, 1979.

Crittenden, Victor H.: *Three Sydney Garden Nurseries in the 1860s*, Mulini Press, Canberra, 1983.

Darlington, H.R.: *Roses*, Jack, London, 1911.

Dyke, Gardiner, Lumley, Spencer: *Trees and Gardens from the Gold Mining Era*, Department of Planning, Melbourne, 1981.

Gibson, Michael: *Shrub Roses, Climbers and Ramblers*, Collins, London, 1973.

Gordon, Lesley: *Poorman's Nosegay*, Collins & Harvihill, London, 1973.

Hole, S. Reynolds: *A Book About Roses*, Edward Arnold, London, 1902.

Howe, George: Observations on Gardening (Australia's first garden guide—1806) reprint, Mulini Press, Canberra, 1980.

Harding, Alice: *Lilacs in My Garden*, Macmillan, New York, 1933.

Harding, Mrs Edward: *The Book of the Peony*, Lippincott, Philadelphia, 1917.

Jekyll, Gertrude: *Colour in the Flower Garden*, Country Life, London, 1908.

Jerkyll, Gertrude: *Wall and Water Gardens* (2nd edition), Country Life, London, 1901.

Jekyll, G., & Mawley, E.: *Roses for English Gardens*, Country Life, London, 1902.

Kelly, Fran: *A Perfumed Garden*, Methuen, Sydney, 1981.

Kelly, Fran: *A Simple Pleasure*, Methuen, Sydney, 1982.

Llewellyn, J., Hudson, B., & Morrison, G.: *Growing Geraniums and Pelargoniums*, Kangaroo Press, Sydney, 1981.

Lloyd, Christopher: *Clematis*, Collins, London, 1977.

McLeod, J.: *The Book of Lavenders*, Wild Woodbine, Bowen Mountain, 1983.

McLeod, J.: *The Book of Sweet Violets*, Wild Woodbine, Bowen Mountain, 1983.

Maeterlinck, Maurice: *Old-Fashioned Flowers*, George Allen & Unwin, London, 1915.

Melliar, Rev. A. Foster: *The Book of the Rose*, Macmillan, London, 1910.

Rohde, Elenor Sinclair: *The Scented Garden*, Medici Society, London, 1931.

Rose, Peter Q.: *Ivies*, Blandford, London, 1980.

Saneki, Kay: *The Fragrant Garden*, Batsford, London, 1981.

Swinbourne, Robert S.: *Years of Endeavour*, S.A. Association of Nurserymen, Adelaide, 1982.

Thomas, Graham Stuart: *The Modern Florilegium*, Sunningdale Nurseries (circa 1950).

Wilder, Louise Beebe: *The Fragrant Path*, Macmillan, New York, 1933.

Wilson, Helen van Pelt, & Bell, Leonie: *The Fragrant Year*, Morrow, New York, 1967.

Wood, Sammuel: *Good Gardening or How to Grow Vegetables, Fruits & Flowers*, Crosby Lockwood & Son, London, 1891.

Catalogues

(and lists consulted in the preparation of this book)

1858   Clifton Nurseries *(Tree list)*, C.M. Ware, North Adelaide, SA

1866   Johnson Rose Nursery, Glenferrie Road North, Hawthorn, Vic.

1876   E. & W. Hacket *(Seed list)*, 73 Rundle Street, Adelaide, SA

1880   E.B. Heyne *(General catalogue)*, Norwood, SA

1894-5   C.F. Newman & Son *(General catalogue)*, Houghton, SA

1898   E. & W. Hacket *(General catalogue)*, Marryatville, SA

1903   D.R. Hunter & Son *(General catalogue)*, 218 Pitt Street, Sydney, NSW

1905   S. Brundrett *(Roses)*, Moonee Ponds, Vic.

INDEX

(Plants listed in the Appendixes are not included in the Index)